Clark College

Court House

Proto-Cathedral

The Academy

Grant House

Public Library

Visitor Center

Esther Short Park

Fort Vancouver

Pearson Air Museum

Waterfront Park

Land Bridge

Patty Grasher

Turtle Place Press

Publisher's Cataloging-in-Publication
(Provided by Cassidy Cataloguing Services, Inc.).
Names: Grasher, Patty, author.

Title: Explore Vancouver Washington / Patty Grasher.

Description: First edition. | Vancouver, WA : Turtle Place Press, [2023]

Identifiers: ISBN: 979-8-218-01343-1 (paperback) | 979-8-9867532-0-1 (ebook)

Subjects: LCSH: Vancouver (Wash.)--Guidebooks. | Vancouver (Wash.)--Description and travel. | Vancouver (Wash.)--History, Local--Guidebooks. | Northwest, Pacific--Guidebooks. | Northwest, Pacific--Description and travel. | Historic sites--Washington (State)--Vancouver--Guidebooks. | Parks--Washington (State)--Vancouver--Guidebooks. | Nature trails--Washington (State)--Vancouver--Guidebooks. | LCGFT: Guidebooks.

Classification: LCC: F899.V2 G73 2023 | DDC: 979.7/86--dc23

Explore Vancouver Washington
Copyright © Patty Grasher 2023

Turtle
Place Press

© 2023 Turtle Place Press - Explore Vancouver USA LLC
6102 NE Hazel Dell Ave
Vancouver WA 98665
360-949-0829
usavancouver.com

SPECIAL SALES
Turtle Place Books are available at special discounts on bulk purchases for corporate, club, or organization sales promotions, premiums and gifts. For more information contact your local bookseller or pat@usavancouver.com
360-949-0829

Fun Facts

WASHINGTON STATE

November 25, 1852 establishment of a new territory north of the Columbia River that included all of present-day Washington, western Idaho and western Montana.

Washington Statehood: Nov 11, 1889 – 42 State (only state named for a U.S. President).

Capital: Olympia

Nickname 1889: The Evergreen State – named for its abundant evergreen forests by C.T. Conover pioneer and Seattle realtor and historian.

Population (2022): 7.8 million
  Seattle 762,687
  Spokane 233,003,
  Tacoma 223,536
  Vancouver 196,739

Abbreviation: WA
State bird:
American Goldfinch
State Flower:
Coast Rhododendron
State insect:
Green Darner Dragonfly

Washington Sales Tax: 6.50% local sales tax max of 4.0%

CLARK COUNTY
Created by the provisional government of Oregon Territory on August 20, 1845 which at that time covered the entire present-day state of Washington.
Population: 2022 - 496,494

VANCOUVER

City Formed:
Population:
1880 - 1,722
1900 - 3,126
1930 - 15,766
1940 - 18,788
1950 - 41,664
1970 - 41,859
1990 - 46,380
2000 - 143,560
2010 - 167,614
2022 - 196,739

Weather: For the most part it is never too hot or cold. Winter lows are in the 40s from December through February with occasional snow surprises lasting a day or two. Summers typical highs are in the 80s with cool nights in the upper 50s with a day or two of rain. Rain average is about 42 inches a year which is about 4 inches above the national average.

City Sales Tax: 8.5 % consists of 6.5% Washington state sales tax +2% Vancouver city tax.

Table of Contents

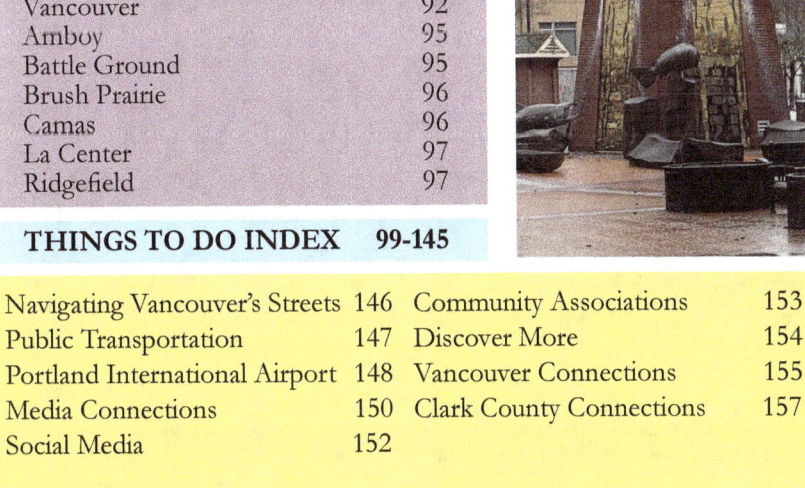

Columbia River

Photo © Jonathon E Kraft

The Columbia starts the first 200 miles of its 1,243-mile journey in British Columbia (BC).

On the American side, the Pend Oreille River joins the Columbia about 2 miles from the Canadian border.

The Columbia receives more than 60 significant tributaries on its path to the Pacific Ocean.

The Columbia empties into the Pacific Ocean just west of Astoria, Oregon. A shifting sandbar at this point makes the river's mouth one of the most hazardous stretches of water to navigate in the world and is often called the "Graveyard of Ships."

In prehistoric times, the Columbia's salmon and steelhead runs numbered an estimated annual average of 10 to 16 million fish, lowering to less than 3.2 million in 1986.

Indigenous peoples have inhabited the Columbia's watershed for more than 15,000 years.

There are 37 known tribes connected to this area, making it one of the highest diversity of indigenous peoples in one area in the world *(see pg 52)*.

Inhabitants of European descent settled here fewer than 230 years ago, beginning with American captain Robert Gray on May 12, 1792. He was the first known explorer to enter the river from the river's mouth.

32 years later in 1825, the Hudson's Bay Company (HBC) established Fort Vancouver on the bank of the Columbia

Facts adapted from Wikipedia Columbia River:

wikipedia.org/wiki/Columbia_River

"May the spirit of the river be the strength of the people"

Quote found at Esther Short Park

Waterfront

The Vancouver Waterfront may have just upped the game for typical before-and-after scenarios. The restoration project begun in 2008 to connect downtown Vancouver to the waterline involved vision and capital funding to the tune of $1.5 billion to transform a historic waterfront eyesore to Cinderella on the Columbia.

Today, there are residential condominiums, hotels, brand-name restaurants, retailers, wine tasting rooms, breweries, a beautiful park, an outdoor amphitheater, and a half-mile of waterfront walkway along the Columbia River. While the Waterfront project is still a work in progress, there is plenty to see, do, and, of course, eat, drink, and be merry in some of the country's top-rated restaurants. The 7-acre Waterfront Park and Grant Street Pier are open to the public from 5am to 10pm.

Limited metered parking is available on weekdays between 7am and 6pm, with additional paid parking lots available and some free street parking nearby.

695 Waterfront Way
visitvancouverwa.com
360-750-1533

Ilchee

Excerpt: In Recognition of the People Who Have Inhabited this Region for Thousands of Years.

Ilchee Moon Girl – "History says she was born along the Columbia River about 1800, daughter of Chinook Chief Concomley and, later, wife of Chief Casinos leader in Vancouver area."
Renaissance Trail - SE Columbia River Dr near Columbia Shores
hmdb.org/m.asp?m=8422

Wendy Rose

A unique tribute honoring women in the workforce at Kaiser during World War II. She was designed and built by six local women welders/artists (Sharon Agnor, Wendy Armstrong, Sumi Wu, Jennifer Corio, Kathy Wilson, Terry Marvin).

The project was sponsored by the City of Vancouver and the Fort Vancouver National Trust.
Columbia River Waterfront near Beaches Restaurant.

Captain George Vancouver Monument Plaza

Photo © Kathleen E. Kraft

Boat of Discovery

Captain George Vancouver
Monument
Excerpt: October 31, 1792 - Lt. William Broughton Named This Area For His Captain

Boat of Discovery
Excerpt: "…The real story of George Vancouver and other explorers of the Pacific Northwest is not in one great voyage. It is in the hundreds of lesser voyages made by the small boats, thoroughness and unfailing courage with which these tasks were carried out through the long years of exploration of the Great River of the West, the Columbia River."
100 Columbia St near 3rd St
hmdb.org/m.asp?m=8516

Captain George Vancouver
1792 Discovery
3 Markers:
Excerpt: "George Vancouver, from King's Lynn, England, at age 35 and with orders from the British Admiralty to explore and chart the West Coast of America, charted hundreds of miles of coast line from California to Alaska."
100 Columbia St near 3rd St
hmdb.org/m.asp?m=8515

Waterfront Markers

A few of the Markers

A Busy Place Is This

Excerpt: "You are standing on the site of a once-bustling river-front complex at Fort Vancouver. A boat building operation, black-smith shop, and tannery filled the air with the sights, sounds, and smells of industry..."

112 Columbia Way
hmdb.org/m.asp?m=12292

A River of Settlers

Excerpt: "Before 1846 American immigrants traveling the Oregon Trail to Fort Vancouver had to make a choice at The Dalles (80 miles upriver from here). They could navigate their own hand-made raft or take a Hudson's Bay Company boat down the Columbia River to here..."

112 Columbia Way
hmdb.org/m.asp?m=12295

Busy Heart of Fort Vancouver

Excerpt: "... ships arrived and de-parted from this bustling port be-ginning in 1825. Ships from Great Britain, the east coast of North America, and the Pacific Islands docked here throughout the 1800s.

112 Columbia Way
hmdb.org/m.asp?m=12292

"The Hudson's Bay Company ship, Beaver, was the first steam-pow-ered ship in the Pacific Northwest, arriving at Fort Vancouver in 1836."

Esther Short Park

Pacific Northwest's First Public Park

The heartbeat of Vancouver pulses from this small, 5-acre park located in downtown Vancouver. Esther Short, one of the area's earliest settlers, donated the land in 1853, thereby establishing the Pacific Northwest's first public park. Her vision for the park was to create a space where all city residents could enjoy the beauty and opportunity of downtown Vancouver.

In the early 1900s, Mayor Royce Pollard kicked off a massive restoration of the park and the city, and private donors have continued to invest and build the park to what it is today.

In addition to the popular weekend Farmer's Market, there is a constant stream of public events, concerts, street musicians, gatherings, public speaking, and an ever active playground for the youth.

W 8th St and Columbia St   cityofvancouver.us   360-487-8311

A Gift For You
by Jim Demetro

"Franklin D. Roosevelt, then candidate for vice president on the Democratic (Cox) ticket, spoke to a "large crowd" in Esther Short park ..."

Aug 21, 1920
Landerholm Chronology

Captain George Vancouver

Captain George Vancouver
By Jim Demetro

The fact is that the naming of Vancouver, Washington was a planned British effort to establish England's presence and first rights to the area by naming it after one of their most famous explorers, Captain George Vancouver in 1824.

The HBC was a powerful fur trade business chartered in 1670. From 1825-1849 Fort Vancouver was the major hub of their export and trade business for the Pacific Northwest. What they accomplished during that short time resulted in many firsts for the Pacific Northwest. *(See timeline pg 53-56).*

It's a common misconception that the city of Vancouver in Washington state was built after the Vancouver in British Columbia.

This 9 foot bronze sculpture by Jim Demetro in 2000 is located at the corner of Sixth and Esther streets near Esther Short Park.

Pioneer Mothers

Excerpt: "After marrying Amos Short in 1829, Esther (Clark) Short set out on the adventure of her life! Originally from Tioga County, Pennsylvania, Esther Short, who was ½ Algonquin Indian, her husband Amos and 10 children traveled west to Linton, Oregon in 1845 and moved again to the present site of downtown Vancouver in 1847..."

Intersection of Columbia St and W 6th St
hmdb.org/m.asp?m=64239

Pioneer Mother
By Avard Fairbanks

Downtown

Farmers Market

The downtown Vancouver Farmers Market comes alive every weekend with over 250 rotating vendors offering a constantly changing display of fresh fruits, vegetables, meats, cheeses, breads, honey, and flowers.

Gorgeous plants from local greenhouses and farms encourage even the most hesitant greenthumb wannabes to try one more time.

Artists, photographers, crafters, jewelry designers, soap makers, and even catnip-treats provide something for everyone. Live music and other entertainers add to the fun.

Open every Saturday and Sunday from late March to the end of October. Go early to avoid the crowd (420,000 shoppers in 2019 pre-Covid) or a bit later to enjoy the hustle, bustle, laughter, and many fresh food enthusiasts pursuing local fruits and veggies.

Corner of Esther St. and W 8th St
vancouverfarmersmarket.com
360-737-8298

Kiggins Theatre

Hats and gloves, while once fashionable attire for attending a Kiggins Theatre event in 1937, are no longer expected, BUT you can still expect to have a wonderful time for the price of a movie ticket in this historic venue.

Listed on the National Register of Historic Places in 2012, the theater moves forward with a blend of old and new architecture, style, and programming that will appeal to all ages.

Purchase tickets online or stand in line like old times and pick up your ticket before entering. Adults can take the experience a step further by ordering a glass of beer, wine, or cider from the Marquee Lounge located inside, and take it to their seat to sip and enjoy during the show.

For more than 80 years, the neon lights of the Marquee have been at the heart of Vancouver community life. Older generations remember

watching their first movie here, later progressing to first dates, date nights, and a night out without the kids.

1011 Main St
kigginstheatre.com
360-816-0352

"The new Kiggins Theatre in Vancouver was dedicated. Its first feature film was "She Married her Boss," staring Claudette Cobert"

Aug 21, 1920
Landerholm Chronology

14

Public Spaces

This book is basically just a sampling, taste and touchpoint of what Vancouver has to offer.

Visit the City's page for public art for more local and unique art pieces.

Download a pdf or visit online
cityofvancouver.us/ourcity/page/public-art

Flying Umbrellas
By Cobalt Designworks

Phrogy

Vancouver public art is a mix of fun, serious, saintly and not so much with surprise bits and pieces tucked in between city streets and plazas.

You can find Phrogy, a hand-carved art piece by an unknown artist on 11th and Broadway.

11th & Broadway.

Waterwheel Replica
Columbia Springs

Clark County Historical Museum

Vancouver has a rich history in the forming and settlement of the American West.

Since 1917, the Clark County Historical Society (CCHS) has worked to collect and preserve the area's historic sites, artifacts, and stories.

Over 60,000 artifacts from the mid-1200s through the present are housed and preserved, though only a small portion are available to the public in its present building, the 1909 Carnegie Library.

Current exhibits cover such topics as Clark County's "Music, Movement and Sound," "History A Brewin'," and "Clark County Stories."

The museum offers
• Guided walking tours,
• History-on-tap events, and
• Digital and Virtual exhibits that are available at any time.

Tue-Sat 11am-4pm and 1st Fri 5pm-8pm

Adults $5, seniors $4, students (18+) $4, children (5-18) $4

Note: With a Vancouver Library card (fvrl.org) you can download a free monthly pass.

1511 Main St
cchmuseum.org
360-993-5679

Providence Academy

The rich history of Providence Academy began with Mother Joseph and four nuns from Montreal who arrived to serve the area's educational, health, social, and religious needs.

The Academy, also called the House of Providence, was the result of prayer, faith, and hard work.

A statue of Mother Joseph was placed in Statuary Hall in the U.S. Capitol as one of the two figures allowed to every state to represent its important history.

Open Mon-Fri 9am-5pm
400 E Evergreen Blvd
thehistorictrust.org
Note: Whe the Academy was built in 1873 by Mother Joseph it was the largest brick building in Washington.

St. James the Greater

This beautiful Roman Catholic Proto-Cathedral of St. James the Greater was built in 1885 by Francois Norbert Blanchet and Modeste Demers.
Gothic Revival architecture.
218 W 12th St
protocathedral.org 360-693-3052

Uptown Village

This historic center of Vancouver honors its past while featuring cozy local shops and businesses tucked in between, like a new flavor of vanilla ice cream on mom's must-eat apple pie.

The words that come to mind to describe Uptown Village is charm, hometown friendliness, and a wonderful place to find something unique and memorable for your first time visit or the hundredth.

Wander through numerous vintage stores, **quaint** boutiques and local shops. Grab a bite from the many restaurants, an ice cream

Photo © Jonathon E Kraft

The Visitor
Artist Matthew Dockrey

Uptown Village is a kaleidoscope of all things magical, fun, and wonderful.

or yogurt spot, or visit Trap Door Brewing, a popular third-generation business that is family friendly until 8pm as well as a number of other family owned businesses.

If you are a bit on the wild side, stop in at Main Street Marijuana, Washington State's largest cannabis retailer.

Don't neglect to get your picture taken next to "The Visitor," a giant steel tentacle (possibly of a dragon or sea monster) slithering from a sewer manhole located at Main St and W 23rd St.
uptownvillage.com

18

Covington House

In 1846, Richard Covington, accompanied by his wife, Anna, arrived from England to take up the position as a teacher for the Hudson's Bay Company.

Both of the Covingtons were teachers, musicians, and artists and brought the first piano into Orgeon Country—along with a violin and guitar.

Their home, built in 1848 (possibly earlier) on Fourth Plain, soon became a center of learning during the day (and boarding school) and a place for lively social gatherings and entertainment for the entire region in the evenings.

From 1852 to 1853, Ullysses S. Grant, a quartermaster at the fort, would often ride over 7 miles to enjoy an evening with the Covingtons.

The couple lived in Vancouver for almost 20 years until 1867 when they departed for Washington, D.C., where the newly elected President Ulysses S. Grant arranged for Richard to work in the Patent Office of the President.

The home fell into disrepair until 1925, when local businessmen raised funds to save and restore the home. It was moved to its present location at 4201 Main St and as one of the oldest buildings in Clark County, it is now a National Landmark.

The house holds monthly "Open House Events" with music and activities.

4201 Main St
covingtonhistorichouse.com

A Few Food Choices

Vancouver offers many delicious food choices. While I would love to share a review of each and every one, time wise that would put the book about two years from tomorrow. So here goes with a startup list of just a few favorites.

Burger

Killer Burger
Mouth-watering, gigantic burgers with home fries that lack moderation in taste and delight. Great vegetarian burgers as well.
616 Northeast 81st St
360-258-1151

1525 SE 164th Ave
360-836-5274

14321 NE Fourth Plain Blvd #102
360-768-5621
killerburger.com

Kitchen Table
Another great breakfast spot that is perfect for larger groups and breakfast meetups. Good service, coffee, food and atmosphere in three locations. While you are making up your mind about what to order, start with their giant fresh baked Cinnamon Roll and share the love.

705 NE 136th Ave Ste 101
360-448-7840

11500 NE 76th St
360-253-8539

1319 NE 134th St Ste 10
360-852-8756
kitchentable-cafe.com

Breakfast

Joe Brown's Cafe
Enjoy casual breakfast and lunch in an old time diner (cooking here since 1932). Voted the best hole in the wall dinner in Washington state in 2023. This is my Sunday (almost every Sunday) place to enjoy a breakfast of fried potatoes and eggs. Very small so you may have trouble getting a seat but great food. Take out & Delivery.
817 Main St
joebrownscafe.com
360-693-6375

Chinese

Golden City
Simply the best hot and sour soup, and after that everything I've tried on the menu is good. It's a small, family owned business that is unpretentious in appearance but delightful for the palette.
Dine-in and take-out.
6204 NE Hwy 99
360-695-9569

Chili

Slow Fox Chili
A small kitchen and bar (but big on taste) in the heart of downtown Vancouver.
108 E 7th St
slowfoxchili.com
360-721-0634

Fish

Northwest Best Fish
Rated the Best Seafood 4 years in a Row in Clark County. Hmmm, must be a reason for that.
Best clam chowder which is high on my list. And if you want to cook your own, their fresh seafood can be shipped directly to your door.
24415 NE 10th Ave Ridgefield
pacificnwbest.com
360-887-4268

Hawaiian

Many people are surprised that Vancouver has a strong Hawaiian presence but we most certainly do. And that presence goes back about 200 years. If you want delicious and authentic Hawaiian fare, here are two great places to try.

Hawaiian Style Grill
Their Huli Huli Chicken and Kal Bi Chicken is "Ono!"
5000 E 4th Plain Blvd A106
hawaiianstylegrill.com
360-993-5306

Hula Boy
Terriyaki Chicken Bento which is also very "Onolicious".
11820 NE Fourth Plain Blvd Ste G
hulaboycharbroil.com
360-896-3355

Mediterranean

Petra House
My bad, but I haven't tried these two places yet but they have great reviews and sounds oh so delicious!
1900 NE 162nd Ave
petrahouserestaurant.com
360-718-7182

George's Molon Lave
and sounds oh so delicous!
1417 SE Rasmussen Blvd #130, Battle Ground
360-687-7770

Fast Mexican

Woody's Tacos
Fresh, authentic Baja style Mexican Cuisine. Sadly there is only outdoor seating but if it's raining just grab, go and devour!
7900 E. Mill Plain Blvd
809 Washington St
360-718-8193

Muchas Gracias
A chain restaurant with 9 locations in Vancouver. Obviously a few folks in town like their food! Offers both dine-in and take out. Fresh, fast and good.
muchasgraciasmexicanfood.com/
locations/washington/vancouver-
locations

Mexican

Los Potrillos
The perfectly cooked Carne Asada is flavorful and delicious. Great place for family, date night or any other excuse you can think of to get there.
10722 NW Lakeshore Ave
360-314-2556

1735 SE 192nd Ave Camas
360-838-2431
lospotrillosweb.com

Sandwich & Sub

Bruchi's Cheesesteaks & Subs
Sometimes you just need a great sub or a nice, drip down, juicy, sandwich.
800 NE Tenney Rd
bruchis.com
360-571-5383

Pizza

Blind Onion
There are just so many good choices for pizza it's hard to pin down just one but the Blind Onion is a good Vancouver first choice with a unique and delicious crust.
blindonionpizza.com
2900 E. Mill Plain Blvd
360-750-7490

9230 NE Hwy 99
360-597-4898

6115 NE 114th Ave #101
360-213-1805

2100 SE 164th Ave A107
360-836-8999

Pizzeria La Sorrentina
Their Neopolitan Pizza is the best, authentic pizza in town.
3000 SE 164th Ave Suite 107
lasorrentinavw.com
360-314-4447

Sushi

Sushi Mo
This choice for sushi is from the high recommendation of a friend who loves sushi. Me not so much but I didn't want to leave it out.
1012 Washington St Ste 140
sushimousa.com
360-953-8860

Thai

Thai Orchard
A popular and busy place with great food. Plan on a wait.
213 West 11th Street
thaiorchidvancouver.us
360-695-7786

Mali Thai Cuisine
Worth the trip from Vancouver.
1251 Lewis River Road Ste B
Woodland
malithaicafe.com
360-841-8043

Ice Cream

Ice Cream Renaissance
Serves homemade ice creams *(gluten and diary free options)*, coffee and locally baked cakes, cookies & pies. Yumfully delicious.
1925 Main St
icecreamrenaissance.square.site
360-694-3892

Yogurt

Yogurt Time
Delicious yogurt and a fun place to stop in while browsing UpTown shops, after a visit to the museum or just because it's time for a Yogurt fix!
1813 Main St
its-yogurt-time.com
360-906-1000

"Let us eat and drink, for tomorrow we diet."

Oregonian - 1908 Guild Cookbook Vancouver, Washington

The Waterfront

The Yard Milkshake Bar
The only thing I tried was a very simple, one scoop ice cream bowl and I've been dreaming about it since. Over-the-top (don't count the calories) delicious.
656 Waterfront way
theyardmilkshakebar.com/vancouver-wa
360-768-9076

Stack571 Whiskey & Burger Bar
Don't let the "whiskey" part stop you from going in as it's definitely family friendly with definitely good food. Do not let the kids know about the milkshakes. Uh, no, not a good idea. Thank you, I will take one though.
670 Waterfront Way
stack571.com
360-450-0774

Waterfront Taphouse
This is one of those places that I keep going back to try more options because they have so much. Deep fried asparagus is definitely one of the winners. A bit spendy but so worth it when you take that first bite. Vegetarian options.
thewaterfronttaphouse.com
360-719-2043

Doomsday Brewing

Erik and Jake have been creating great craft beer in Clark County since 2012.

doomsdaybrewing.com
1919 Main Street
360-503-7649

9301 NE 5th Ave Ste 120
360-559-8241

421 C St Unit 3 Washougal
360-335-9909

Heathen Brewing Feral Public House

Another popular choice.
1109 Washington Street
heathenbrewing.com/feral-public-house
360-836-5255

There are many more excellent craft brews throughout the city.
visitvancouverwa.com/food-drink/breweries-and-tap-houses

Amaro's Table

Good food, good ambience, good drinks. Dine-in & Takeout.
1220 Main St. Ste. 100   360-718-2942
816 NE 98th Cir.   360-718-7046
amarostable.com

Billygan's Roadhouse

Comfortable, and casual dining atmosphere with great food (best rolls and honeybutter). Good choice for families or best buds night. Generous Happy Hour specials.
13200 NE Hwy 99
billygansroadhouse.com
360-573-2711

Frontier Public House

Their websites states that their food is "tasty made-from-scratch Southern inspired comfort food," all I know is that their Chicken N Dumplings are just way too good. Dine-in & Takeout.
4909 NE Hazel Dell Ave
facebook.com/frontierpublichouse
360-718-2768

This page purposely left blank to add your favorites.

Events by the Month

JANUARY

Jan 16 Free Day at Fort Vancouver

FEBRUARY

Valentine's Ball

MARCH

Farmers Market

APRIL

Sakura Festival
Apr 22 Free Day at Fort Vancouver

MAY

Cedar Creek Grist Mill Bread & Butter Day
Hazel Dell Parade of Bands - 3rd Sat May
Lilac Days at Hulda Klager Gardens
Memorial Day Celebration at Vancouver Barracks

JUNE

Camas Classic Car Show
Pomeroy Living History Farm Days (Jun-Aug)
Tacos in the Park

JULY

4 Days of Aloha
Craft Beer & Wine Fest
Friday Night Movies in the Park
Saturday in the Park Pride
Summer Fest - 4th of July Celebrations
Territorial Days - Amboy
WWII Encampment at the Fort

REPEATING EVENTS

Cedar Creek Grist Mill Events - Saturdays
Chelatchie Prairie Train Rides
Spirit Tales of the Vancouver Barracks - July thru Halloween

Check these online Event Calendars for current updates
visitvancouverwa.com/events cityofvancouver.us/calendar

Events by the Month

AUGUST

Clark County Fair
Heritage Garden Party
Vancouver Brewfest
Sunflower Festivals
Aug 4 Free Day at Fort Vancouver

SEPTEMBER

Harvest Days & Pumpkin Patch
Sunflower Festivals
Sep 23 Free Day at Fort Vancouver

OCTOBER

Apple Cider Pressing
Birdfest & Bluegrass
Dine the Couve
Harvest Days & Pumpkin Patch
Haunted Walking Tour
Oktoberfests
Pumpkin Lane Pomeroy Farms

NOVEMBER

Bazaars, Holiday Markets
Chelatchie Prairie Fall Train Rides
Community Tree Lighting
Native American Event at Fort Vancouver
Pow Wow at Clark College
Nov 11 Free Day at Fort Vancouver

DECEMBER

Bazaars, Holiday Markets
Christmas Ships
Community Chanukah Celebration
Noel Vancouver
Santa Train

EVERY MONTH

First Friday Art Walk - Vancouver
Camas First Friday
Comedy on Tap - 2nd Thursday

Check these online Event Calendars for current updates
events.columbian.com   clarkcoeventcenter.com/events

Events A-Z

4 Days of Aloha - Multi-celebration of Hawaiian arts and culture with activities such as Hula & Craft Workshops, Pā'ina Concert in the Park, Hō'ike, and the Aloha Fun Run. Jul - Thu-Sun **Esther Short Park**
4daysofaloha.com

Apple Cider Pressing - Kids can work hand-cranked presses to turn apples into mouth-watering nectar. Bluegrass Jam music. Last Sat Oct, opens 9am Free - **Cedar Creek Grist Mill**
cedarcreekgristmill.org

Bazaars, Holiday Markets - These events change often check the links below for latest updates.
Columbian columbian.com/holiday-spot
Clark County Talk clarkcountytalk.com
Visit Vancouver Washington
visitvancouverwa.com/events/seasonal-events/

Birdfest & Bluegrass - Celebrate the annual return of the sandhill cranes with music, crafts, food, and birding activities. Oct - check website
Ridgefield
ridgefieldfriends.org/birdfest-bluegrass

Camas Classic Car Show - Held the last Saturday of June. $20 for car entry with no pre-registration necessary. Raffles, live music, dance and other family friendly entertainment. 2-7pm free for spectators.
downtowncamas.com/event/camas-car-show

Camas First Friday - Community events that happen the first Friday of every month from 5-8pm. Activities, art, dining, and after hours shopping.
downtowncamas.com/events-and-festivals/first-fridays

Cedar Creek Grist Mill Events -
Check website for events such as Apple Cider Pressing, Bread & Butter Days, Strawberry Shortcake Days and more.
43907 NE Grist Mill Road - Woodland, WA
cedarcreekgristmill.org/index.php/events
360-225-5832

Chelatchie Prairie Train Rides -
All aboard for a great time. Sat & Sun - see website for times and fares.
207 Railroad Ave, Yacolt, WA
tickets.bycx.org
360-686-3559

Christmas Ships - Begun in 1954, the Christmas Ships are currently a
fleet of 55 to 60 boats up and down the Columbia. 15 days in Dec.
Find an open spot along the river or take it up a notch with a hotel and
dining reservation at Waterfront eateries (plan ahead up to a year in
advance).
christmasships.org

Clark County Fair - Ten days of fair exhibits, contests, music and fun
that starts on the first Friday in August.
clarkcofair.com
564-397-6180

Comedy on Tap - 90 minutes of comedy for your laughing pleasure.
Every second Tuesday at **Kiggins Theatre**.
1011 Main St   Cost: $15 Time: 8pm
kigginstheatre.com/eventscomedy-on-tap
360-816-0352

Community Chanukah Celebration - Lighting of the Grand Me-
norah, entertainment, and donuts to celebrate the Jewish holiday season.
1st evening of Chanukah 4:30pm - Free - **Esther Short Park**
jewishvancouverwa.com

Community Tree Lighting -
The tree lighting ceremony is held the Friday after Thanksgiving. The
tree remains lighted until New Year's Day.
Esther Short Park
rotarytreelighting.org

Craft Beer & Wine Fest - 3 days of live music and fun at Beer Village, Wine Country, and Whiskey Town. Pet friendly. See website for
hours. Presales **and** at door - **Esther Short Park**
thecraftwinefest.com

Dine the Couve - October is Vancouver's Official Dining Month. Restaurants sign up to provide special menu offers at $25 or $35 for three items. A unique and delightful way to discover new restaurants and support local business.
visitvancouverwa.com/dinethecouve

Dozer Days - Held in October
Construction Junction for kids at the Clark County Convention Center. Kids climb into the driver's seat of heavy construction equipment, fire engines, and even an ambulance with education about building sustainable communities, industry opportunities, and public safety.
17402 NE Delfel Rd, Ridgefield, WA
vancouver.dozerday.org

Farmers Market -
Downtown Market 8th & Esther St (mid Mar - Oct)
East Vancouver Market 17701 SE Mill Plain Blvd (mid Jun - Aug)
Fall Market 8th & Esther St 8th & Esther St (Nov - mid Dec)
vancouverfarmersmarket.com

First Friday Camas - Family community event in Camas with after-hours shopping, art exhibits, monthly featured activities, and dining.
1st Fri every month 5pm-8pm - Free
downtowncamas.com/events-and-festivals/first-Fridays

First Friday Downtown Art Walk - featuring rotating exhibits from local artists. 1st Fri every month 5pm-9pm - Free - Downtown Vancouver vdausa.org/events

Friday Night Movies in the Park - Each week, a different movie at a different park. Bring seating. Jul-mid-Aug, starting at 9pm-9:30pm - Free
cityofvancouver.us/parksrecculture/page/friday-night-movies-parks

Haunted Walking Tour - October
Sponsored by the Clark County Historical Museum this is a fun mile walking tour along Main Street. Starts at 6pm every Fri & Sat in October. Tickets for ages 6 and up are $18. Best suited for ages 10 and up.
cchmuseum.org/programs-events/haunted-walking-tours

Harvest Days & Pumpkin Patch - (Clark County)

Local Farms provide Pumpkin Plunkin Fun.
Check websites for dates and locations near you.

Bi-Zi Farms - 9504 NE 119th St
bizifarms.com

Vancouver Pumpkin Patch - at Velvet Acres Gardens
18905 NE 83rd St
vancouverpumpkinpatch.com

The Patch -
612 Whalen Rd Woodland, WA
avidgardener.webs.com

Pumpkin Lane - at Pomeroy Farms
20902 NE Lucia Falls Rd Yacolt, WA
pomeroyfarm.org

Thiselle Creek Farm -
26903 NE CC Landon Rd Yacolt, WA
thisellecreekfarm.com

Walton Farms -
1617 NE 267th AVE Camas, WA
waltonsfarms.com

Hazel Dell Parade of Bands - 28 high school bands, 100 floats, ponies, fire trucks, and clowns. 3rd Sat May (Armed Forces Day) - Free
NE Hwy 99 and Hazel Dell Ave
hdscba.org/parade

Heritage Garden Party - Friends of Fort Vancouver celebrate the annual fort harvest with a wine and beer garden event. Visit with volunteer gardeners sharing historic garden and preservation tips.
friendsfortvancouver.org

Juneteenth - Celebrate freedom with history, art, and up to 70 vendor tables for shopping, resources, and employment opportunities for all.
1pm-7pm - Free - Esther Short Park
juneteenthfreedomcelebration.com

Lilac Days at Hulda Klager Gardens -
Nonprofit botanical gardens specializing in lilacs. Lilac Days are open for 23 days leading up to Mother's Day. The gardens are open daily 10:00 a.m. until 4:00 p.m. year around for a $4 gate fee.
lilacgardens.com

Farm Days at Pomeroy Living History Farm
The first weekend of the months June-August is open farm weekend, featuring the historic grounds, farm animals, iSpy children's activity, and many local artisans and vendors. Suggested donation is $3 per person, or $15 per family. 11am-5pm. Pets allowed only in parking area.
20902 NE Lucia Falls Rd Yacolt, WA
pomeroyfarm.org

Memorial Day Celebration at the Fort - Vancouver's annual Memorial Day Observance held at 11am on Monday at the bandstand parade with keynote speaker, color guard, release of doves, and free lunch. Memorial Day - Free - **Fort Vancouver NHS**, 1501 E Evergreen Blvd
nps.gov/fova/index.htm

Native American Arts and Salmon Festival - Meet regional Native American artists and peruse their prints, jewelry and sculptures. Free event from 10am - 4pm at Fort Vancouver Visitor Center.
friendsfortvancouver.org/events

Pow Wow at Clark College - First weekend of November. Blessing and Welcome at 5pm followed by the Pow Wow Grand Entry at 6pm. The evening continues with a celebration of music, dance and food. Free and open to community. Gaiser Student Center Main Campus
clark.edu/campus-life/arts-events/native-american/index.php

Sakura Festival - Opening remarks take place at 1:00 p.m. in the Royce Pollard Japanese Friendship Garden Celebration begins at 2:30 p.m. in Clark College Gaiser Student Center.
clark.edu/campus-life/arts-events/sakura/index.php

Saturday in the Park Pride - Celebrate the lives and history of the LGBTQ. Community in SW Washington.
Esther Short Park - 2nd Sat in July 7:30 am Free
vanusapride.org

Spirit Tales of the Vancouver Barracks - Jul-Oct 31 -
Guided walking tour by local historian and author Jefferson Davis at the
historic Vancouver Barracks. Tickets $12-$18. See website.
ghostsandcritters.com

Summer Fest - 4th of July Celebrations - An all-ages event with live
music, games, history tours of military vehicles, beer & cider tastings, and
outdoor film screening (bring a blanket). BBQ and favorite summertime
food. 11 am 1st Sun Jul - Free - Parade Grounds and Officers Row
thehistorictrust.org/calendar/summer-fest

Sunflower Festival Bi-Zi Farms - Ticket includes a free hayride, one
cut sunflower and a chance to visit with adorable animals at their petting
zoo.
Check website for dates and ticket information.
bi-zifarms.com

Sunflower Festival O'Keefe Farms - Admission includes three u-cut
flowers and unlimited time to stroll the sunflower fields and take pictures.
Artisan vendors, food truck and Smokin' Franks Barbecue. Live music.
No pets. Check website for dates and ticket information.
okeefeflowerfarm.com/home-maple

Tacos in the Park - Add tacos, brews, cider, and tequila blended with
live music and video arcade, and you're ready for fun. Jun - check website
Esther Short Park - $20 - $500 supports the local ARC foundation.
recycledartsfestival.com

Territorial Days at Amboy - July
Community event open to all featuring logging skills, parade, cruise-in,
vendors, artisans and family fun activities.
tdays.org

Valentine's Ball - Celebrate the love of your child's birth, adopted or
chosen family in a welcoming environment. A time for wonderful memo-
ries, music and dancing at the Annual Valentine's Day Ball.
Historic Hangar at Pearson Air Museum
cityofvancouver.us/parksrecculture/page/valentine's-ball

Vancouver Summer Brewfest - August

Features 40 Washington breweries, live music, vendors and fun at Esther Short Park for two days in August. Admission includes eight 5-ounce tastes and a souvenir glass.

washingtonbeer.com/festivals/vancouver-summer-brewfest.php

Wine & Jazz Festival - The No. 1 cultural tourism event in Southwest Washington with Grammy Award-winning, internationally acclaimed musicians, regional jazz, and blues bands; Northwest wines; fine artists; and local cuisine. Aug - check website for times. **Esther Short Park** - Day pass ($25 advance)$35 Weekend Pass $80

vancouverwinejazz.com

World War II Encampment - Two day reenactment portraying members of various U.S. Army units from World War II as well as workers on the home front. Hosted by the Living History Group Northwest.

Fort Vancouver National Historic Site.

Check website for dates.

lhgnw.org

This page purposely left blank to add your own notes.

Cedar Creek Grist Mill

Photo © Jonathon E Kraft

The Cedar Creek Grist Mill originally the Red Bird Mill was built in 1876 by miller, George Woodham and his sons.

1961 it was listed as a Historical Place and is now a complete working museum using only water power for running the mill and lights.

Volunteers trained and dressed as millers explain the history and show the inside workings of a grist mill as it would have been operated in 1876.

Special events throughout the year with the big time favorite Apple Cider Pressing in October.

Saturday 1 - 4 p.m.
43907 NE Grist Mill Rd Woodland,
cedarcreekgristmill.org
360-225-5832

Baking Powder Biscuit

1 quart flour　　　　　　　　1 level teaspoon salt
1 pint fresh milk　　　　　　2 heaping tablespoons lard
2 heaping teaspoons baking powder

Sift flour, baking powder and salt, three times, add milk and mix lightly with spoon, (do not use hands.) Pour over this the lard melted and hot. Mix, turn on well-floured board, spread with fingers, cut, turn in hot lard or butter, and immediately place in hot oven and bake fifteen minutes.

-- Mrs. F. E HODGKIN.
1908 Guild Cookbook - Vancouver, Washington

Chelatchie Prairie Railroad

Dial back 100 years or so and you can catch a ride on the Chelatchie Prairie train that will transport you through Clark County countryside from Yacolt to Moulton Falls to Chelatchie Prairie and back.

This no-frills ride is for hardy and fun, adventure-seeking travelers who are not afraid of murder mysteries, train hold-ups, and possibly a rare glimpse of a Sasquatch.

Seating available on open sided cars (benches are hard, bring a small pillow to sit on) or travel in style in the enclosed coach. Either way this is a fun not-to-be missed time for all ages.

Trains run an average of every other weekend during the May-Dec. season. Check the website bycx.com for details and to make reservations.

207 Railroad Ave, Yacolt
facebook.com/ChelatchiePrairieRailroad
360-686-3559

Ridgefield Wildlife Refuge

Birdsong and rustling breezes break up the silence along quiet trails that invite you to step softly and enjoy deeply along this beautiful nature walk.

Over 5,000 acres of wetlands, grasslands, vegetation, and forests provide safe places for songbirds, wintering waterfowl, and other local native species. An auto tour route allows for easy viewing while protecting vulnerable species.

Plan to visit during different times of the year, as each season showcases its own natural splendor. **Entrance pavilion**, **Spur Trail**, and **Lake River** overlook are free.

Access hours daily 6am-8:30pm Refuge Office

Check website for seasonal closure, day and one year passes.

ridgefieldfriends.org

360-887-4106

Carty Unit
Pedestrian Entrance
Daily 6am-8:30pm
May 1-Sept 30
28908 NW Main Ave, Ridgefield
Access to Refuge Office, Cathlapotle Plankhouse, Oaks-to-Wetlands Trail, and the seasonal Carty Lake Trail
Oct-Apr

River S Unit
Auto Tour Route
This entrance allows for year-round access by car, the seasonal Kiwa trail, and the seasonal waterfowl hunting program. There are two sets of waterless, non-flush toilets with no running water.
1071 S Hillhurst Rd, Ridgefield

Cathlapotle Plankhouse

Chinookans built one-roofed, multiple dwellings called plank-houses as far back as the mid-1300s. It took as many as 100 trees and 2,000 person hours to build a single house over a course of several years.

By the time the Lewis and Clark expedition showed up in 1805, one of the largest villages had as many as 14 plankhouses.

Thirty-five years later, white man's diseases wiped out entire villages, and the houses disappeared.

This reconstructed plankhouse is an interpretive center used by the Chinook Indian Nation.

Currently the plankhouse is not open to public viewing but one can stroll past it and see it in a natural setting as it would have been for thousands of years.

See Ridgefield Wildlife Refuge for location.

ridgefieldfriends.org/plankhouse
facebook.com/ridgefieldfriends

"The Cathlapotle Plankhouse is sacred to our tribal communities. Please do not climb on it, remove wood, or otherwise damage it, thank you."

North Clark Historical Museum

While every person "has a story," so does every community whether large or small. The town of Amboy's population is just a breath over 1,000, but the community spirit is strong, and this small museum is avid testimony of that.

After the fur trade diminished in the late 1800s, logging became the new moneymaker. Amboy among other things was a logging town, and that history is told here along with Native American culture and pioneer stories.

2nd and 4th Sat 12pm-4pm
21416 399th St / Jct of SR 503, Amboy
northclarkhistoricalmuseum.org

Two Rivers Heritage Museum

One of the newest museums in Clark County is stepping up into a popular tourist attraction.

Covering the full scope of the area's events, people, and industry, it includes the Pendleton weaving mill, which started in 1912, and the latest attraction, a Native American exhibit called the "Washuxwal Gathering Place."

A few collections not to be missed include early American toys, kitchen ware (with one of the oldest kitchen stoves in the country), music, and work tools.

Sat 11am-3pm Mar–Oct
Adults $5, seniors $2, students $2
Group tours by appt: $8
1 Durgan St, Washougal
2rhm.com
360-835-8742

Take a Tour

Land Bridge

A 1/3 mile, self guided walk over a bridge connecting Vancouver Waterfront Park to the Fort Vancouver National Historic Site. The location was chosen to mark a cultural and spiritual symbolic area of Pacific Northwest Native Americans. See (pages 26-27)

City of Vancouver

Heritage Tree Tour

Self-guided tour of 16 historic trees or groves that have been designated as Vancouver Heritage Trees. Spread across 13 parks and public locations throughout the city.

cityofvancouver.us/publicworks/page/self-guided-heritage-tree-tour

Ghost Walks

"Spirit Tales of the Vancouver Barracks" haunted walking tours take place from July through Halloween. Contact Jeff Davis
General Tickets: $18
Senior (60+) $12.
Veteran $12.
Youth (15 and younger) $12.
ghostsandcritters.com/main.html
253 223-0125

Historic Trust

Botanical Walking Tour

This self-guided tour explores plantings along Officers Row and the surrounding area.
thehistorictrust.org/self-guided-tours

Providence Academy Tours

Built in 1873 by Mother Joseph, an architect, carpenter and religious nun. Open for tours by reservation or walk-in.
Wed-Fri 10am-2pm
thehistorictrust.org/tours
360-992-1800

Marshall House Tours

Walk-in tours.
Wed-Fri 10am-2pm
thehistorictrust.org/tours
360-992-1800

National Park Service

The Spruce Mill Trail

Self-guided outdoor tour.

During World War I extensive amounts of lumber was needed to build airplanes. Operated by the Spruce Production Division (U.S. Army) this mill was the largest of its kind in the world with almost 30,000 soldiers assigned to meet the demand.

nps.gov/thingstodo/walkingspruce.htm

Vancouver Barracks

Self-guided tour of the first U.S. Army post in the Pacific Northwest. *(See pg 70-82)*

The post served as a major headquarters and supply depot during the Civil War and Indian War eras and later as a recruitment, mobilization and training facility for the Spanish-American War, the Philippine War and other foreign engagements.

nps.gov/fova/learn/historyculture/vb.htm

nps.gov/places/vancouverbarracks.htm

Hudson Bay Company (HBC) at Fort Vancouver NHS

Ranger-led tours (subject to Ranger availability) are once or twice a day normally at 10a.m. and 2p.m. Call ahead. Best days to visit are Friday and Saturday between 9am-2pm when the most reenactors will be there but it is definitely a fun self-guided visit as well.

1501 E Evergreen Blvd

nps.gov/fova/learn/historyculture/hbcfort1.htm

Self-guided tours with interpretive panels in front of buildings, landmarks, and pathways.

Pearson Air Museum

(See pg 82-83)

Self-guided. Explore local aviation history at the Museum and Jack Murdock Aviation Center. It began as a military air field in the early 1900s with significant contributions through two world wars and other historic events.

nps.gov/fova/planyourvisit/pearsonairmuseum.htm

Columbia River Cruises

American Queen Voyages

A nine-day cruise along the Columbia River from Vancouver to Clarkston, Washington.

americansteamboatcruises.co.uk

Portland Spirit

A variety of cruises offered, including brunch, lunch, dinner, "Heart of Portland," and dance.

Brunch Cruise | Lunch Cruise | Dinner Cruise | Heart of Portland | Dance Cruise

portlandspirit.com

Scovare Expeditions

A variety of sailing and power-boat tours, including Christmas ships, private boat cruise, private powerboat cruise, private yacht cruise.

Christmas Ships Cruise | Private Sailboat Cruise | Private Power-boat Cruise | Private Yacht Cruise

sailscovare.com

Willamette Jetboat Excursions

One-, two-, and three-hour cruises, three-hour lunch tour.

willamettejet.com

Columbia River Renaissance Trail

Photo © Jonathon E Kiat

Ilchee - Artist Eric Jensen

Wendy Rose - Six Local Women Welders/ Artists (Sharon Agnor, Wendy Armstrong, Sumi Wu, Jennifer Corio, Kathy Wilson, Terry Marvin)

You cannot validate your experience of Vancouver until you have visited bits, pieces, or all of the Columbia River Renaissance Trail.

This easily accessible, 14-foot-wide concrete path winds along the Columbia River shoreline for a little over 5 miles, passing monuments, sculptures, historic landmarks, and parks.

It offers spectacular views of the river and Oregon's second highest mountain, Mount Hood. Ducks, geese, heron, and other water-fowl float happily along the flowing current looking for tasty fish tidbits and nibbles.

Boats large and small continue their busy journeys up and down the river, while a wide assemblage of aircraft, from twin-prop propelled motion from Pearson Field, fly below the full-thrust airways of military and commercial jets from larger airfields on the Oregon side.

It's a touchpoint for all things old and new, a thread of pavement that links to the latest architecture of today and just as swiftly thrusts you hundreds of years back into Vancouver's earliest days with the reconstruction of the Hudson Bay's Company most prestigious Fort Vancouver.

Columbia Way
cityofvancouver.us
360-487-8311

Discovery Loop Historic Trail

Start your exploration of Vancouver with this easy 2.3-mile loop that leads you through significant points in Vancouver's history.

Esther Short Park – the oldest public square in the state of Washington.

Providence Academy - a former orphanage and school built in 1873 by Mother Joseph of the Sacred Heart.

Old Apple Tree Park – the first apple tree planted in Washington State.

Confluence Land Bridge – reopens a path once used by ancient Native Americans

Historic Fort Vancouver – the reconstructed fort of the Hudson's Bay Company.

Vancouver Barracks – the first U. S. Army presence in the Pacific Northwest and the first PX established in the United States.

Officers Row on E Evergreen Blvd – the largest reconstruction of historic officers housing in the country.

Pearson Air Museum – the first air commercial field in the Pacific Northwest, considered the country's oldest continuously operating airfield.

Lieutenant Broughton, sent by Capt. Vancouver, was abreast of the site of Vancouver -- the first white man definitely known to have been there. By canoe.

Oct 29, 1792
Landerholm Chronology

Confluence Land Bridge

Dedicated August 2008

This place along the river has been a historic crossroads for Native people, and later for Lewis and Clark, the Hudson's Bay Company, and now Fort Vancouver. Today, the Confluence Land Bridge crosses over the highway to reconnect people with the river.

John Paul Jones and Jones Architects designed the Land Bridge with artistic consultation by celebrated artist Maya Lin. Indigenous plants, native languages, and basket-weaving patterns reveal insights about the confluence of the land, the river, and the people. The Welcome Gate, designed by artist Lillian Pitt, honors the Chinookan women who played an integral role in shaping this place.

The Confluence Land Bridge is one of six Confluence sites connected to the Columbia River system. Confluence is a community-supported nonprofit that connects people to place through art and education.

1 – Welcome Gate

The Welcome Gate, by artist Lillian Pitt, greets visitors by representing and honoring the way Chinookan people welcome visitors arriving by canoe. Two cedar logs are topped with crossed canoe paddles, set with the cast-glass face of a Chinookan woman.

2 – Overlooks

Three overlooks on the bridge mark the locations of the river, prairie, and village. Spirit Baskets by Lillian Pitt feature figures inspired by Columbia River petroglyphs. The words for River, Land, and People appear in nine Native languages on stainless-steel panels.

3 – Ethnobotancial Walkway

Until the 17th century, the landscape was a patchwork of prairie, forest, and wetlands. Native plant species from these distinct habitats are now showcased along the Land Bridge walkway, identified by a series of interpretative panels.

The Confluence Land Bridge is a 40-foot-wide, earth-covered pedestrian bridge that reconnects a time-honored path to the river disrupted by a major state highway. It is one of six interpretive art landscapes created along 438 miles of the Columbia River by the Confluence Project.

The bridge is an educational experience linking the history, living culture, and ecology of the area from indigenous peoples to the people living here today.

South entrance: To access the bridge, you can start from the Old Apple Tree Park along the Renaissance Trail and walk under the overpass to the Welcome Gate.

North entrance: From I-5, take Mill Plain east, turn right at Fort Vancouver Way, and continue through the roundabout. Turn left and park on E 5th St. The path to the Confluence Land Bridge will be on your right.

confluenceproject.org
360-693-0123
Text from interpretative panel

48

Burnt Bridge Creek Trail

Location of "possibly the first bridge built in Washington State."
pacific-hwy.net/burnt.htm

The Hudson's Bay Company built a simple wood bridge across this creek around the late 1830s to transport produce on ox carts. Because it was the only bridge in the area to connect between the northern prairies and Fort Vancouver, it was simply called Bridge Creek.

Since that time, the bridge underwent a number of name changes until it burned down sometime after 1860 and, though a new bridge was built, the name Burnt Bridge Creek stuck. In 1897, the U.S. Board of Geographic Names made the name Burnt Bridge Creek official.

The Burnt Bridge Creek Trail is a shared-use, paved trail that is great for walking, biking, and jogging. While the full length of the trail is 8 miles, it is easy to break into smaller routes. Downloadable maps for western, central, and eastern sections are available from cityofvancouver.us.

The full trail runs from Vancouver Lake at Stewart's Glen in the Fruit Valley Neighborhood to NE 97th Ave between 18th St and NE 16th St.

cityofvancouver.us
(parks and trails)

> Lewis and Clark visited the site of Vancouver.
>
> *Nov. 4, 1805*
> *Landerholm Chronology*

Salmon Creek Greenway

A simple, 3.1-mile paved pathway makes an easy walk and nature break along a beautiful waterway that is home to year-round birds, migratory waterfowl, deer, coyotes, rabbits, opossums, raccoons, and beavers.

A small portion of the walk shows a few houses offset from the trail, but mostly it is a wooded area with small fields that wind along the way rich with birdsong, wildflowers, and the sweet nature aromas of woods, water, and plant growth.

This is a lovely path for walkers, joggers, and parents with baby strollers. Bikes are allowed, though I have yet to see them, and dogs are also allowed if leashed.

There are two entry points for the walk, with the main entrance at Salmon Creek Klineline Pond requiring a vehicle parking fee on weekdays (though you can go a bit west of the lot to the recreation center parking lot and park for free). The other trailhead site provides free off-highway parking along N 36th Ave.

NW 36th Ave

No entrance fee, but there is a daily parking fee at Klineline Pond.
Annual parking permit: $30

clark.wa.gov/public-works/parking-fees

Columbia Springs Trail

Photo © Jonathan E Kraft

Two miles of trails wind through 100 acres of forested green, two lakes, and wildlife, and along the historic Vancouver Trout Hatchery, fish-feeding pond, and two wildlife viewing areas.

Along the way, art, interpretive signage, and historical displays such as the historic waterwheel replica are all part of this nature-enriched environment.

The ADA-accessible Visitor Center is open daily from dawn to dusk for free. Dogs on leash are permitted.

Field trips for school children, guided hikes, tours, fairs, and festivals are all part of the year-round activities.

12208 SE Evergreen Hwy
columbiasprings.org
360-882-0936

Photo © Jonathan E Kraft

Tsi-nuk (Chinook) Peoples

The area around Vancouver and the Columbia River until the arrival of Europeans had a long tradition of being a trading center for American Indians for thousands of years. Chinook Indians who lived in this area traded among different nearby tribes as well as those who traveled hundreds of miles during the summer months to trade and fish.

Cascades
Californian
Carrier
Cayuse
Chaudieres
Chehalis
Chinook
Clallam
Cowichan
Cowlitz
Cree
Delaware
Grande Dalles
Haida
Iroquois
Kalapuya
Kalama
Kathlamet
Mollala
Mowatwos
Nez Perce
Nipissing
Nisqually
Okanagan
Pend d'Oreille
Rogue
Shasta
Snake
Shohomish
Spokane
Stikine
Tillamook
Tsnoomus
Umpqua
Walla Walla

Spirit Pole - Toma Villa
Fort Vancouver Visitor Center

Time Line

2000 BC to Present – **Chinook Indians** consisting of 37 known tribes live or trade along the lower Columbia River near present-day Vancouver.

Skichutxwa was the first name for the area of Vancouver.

1579 Great Britain – Sir Francis Drake may explore the Washington coast.

1592 Spanish – Greek navigator Juan de Fuca may enter the fabled "Northwest Passage" during a Spanish expedition.

1792 American – The first contact with Natives possibly takes place when Robert Gray enters the "Great River of the West" aboard the Columbia Rediviva.

Spanish – The Spanish sail from Mexico to explore the North American coast and "recorded rapid and abundant river," probably describing the mouth of the Columbia River.

1792 Great Britain – Lieutenant William Broughton under orders from Captain George Vancouver explores the Columbia River and makes contact with indigenous tribes.

1800 First recorded eruption of Mount St. Helens.

1805 and 1806 American – The Lewis and Clark Expedition travels through Clark County.

1818 Great Britain and United States Treaty of Joint Occupation.

1821 Hudson's Bay Company buys out Northwest Company.

1825 Great Britain – Hudson's Bay Company (HBC) moves headquarters from Astoria to Vancouver.

1826 Great Britain – HBC plants the first apple tree in the Pacific Northwest and many other crops.

1836 First steamboat on the Columbia River (The Beaver) arrives at Fort Vancouver.

1841 American – Commander Charles Wilkes leads the United States Exploring Expedition to explore the Columbia River.

1843 American – Dr. John McLoughlin at Fort Vancouver saves from starvation the first wagon train to reach Vancouver on the way to Oregon. He acts against HBC's policy of not aiding the Americans.

1845 – Amos and Esther Short accused of murdering landholder and claimed land owned by HBC.

1845 – The provisional government of Oregon creates Clark County, which then covered the entire state of Washington. It is named after William Clark of the Lewis and Clark Expedition.

1846 – Treaty of 1846 formalizes the border between the United **States** and British North America west of the Rocky Mountains. The HBC presence moves permanently to B.C. above the 49th parallel.

1849 – **U.S. Army arrives** to settle Indian Uprisings (Camp Vancouver) and provide for American settlement. The first officer quarters are built along Evergreen Ave.

1850-1853 – Camp Vancouver renamed Columbia Barracks.

1852 – Ulysses S. Grant, a lieutenant and quartermaster with the 4th Infantry, serves at Columbia Barracks.

1853 – Columbia Barracks renamed Fort Vancouver.

1855 – Mrs. Short builds steamboat landing and donates Esther Short Park and a long strip of waterfront perpetually.

1856 – Mother Joseph arrives at Vancouver

1857 – City of Vancouver is incorporated and the first mayor, Levi Farnsworth, is elected.

1860 Great Britain – The HBC abandons Fort Vancouver.

1861 – Vancouver Barracks becomes a major headquarters and supply depot during the Pacific Northwest Indian War era and the Civil War.

1866 – Mysterious fire starting from 12 different places at once burns the HBC Fort Vancouver to the ground. 500 soldiers stand by watching it burn.

1870s – Reigns as Prune Capital of the World until the 1930s.

1873 – Sisters of Providence build an academy to schoolchildren of the territory, including orphans.

1877 – General O. O. Howard and Nez Perce War of 1877.

1877-78 – 33 members of Nez Perce Chief Redheart's band is captured under the direction of General O. O. Howard and held unjustly as prisoners at Fort Vancouver, with one infant dying during this time (see year 1998).

1878 – General O. O. Howard and the Paiute Bannock War of 1878.

1879 – Fort Vancouver renamed Vancouver Barracks.

1885 – General Gibbon at Fort Vancouver is given command of the Department of the Columbia. Gibbon's troops restore order in Seattle when wracked by anti-Chinese turmoil.

1889 – Chief Joseph visited and stayed with Brigadier General John Gibbon at his home on Vancouver Barracks' Officers' Row (now known as Marshall House).

1901 – First Oregon and Washington railway train (Northern Pacific Railway) entered Vancouver.

1905 – Lincoln Beachey flies a dirigible from the Portland fairgrounds to Vancouver Barracks.

1906 – The first large ship, Steamboat Thyra docks at Vancouver.

1908 – First major railroad, North Bank Railroad, reached Vancouver.

1908 – Columbian became Clark County's first daily newspaper.

1910 – Aviation began at what is now Pearson Field with dirigible landing.

1912 – Vancouver passed vote to establish Port of Vancouver.

1917 – Spruce Lumber Mill under the U.S. Army oversaw 30,000 workers to produce lumber for thousands of planes to fight in World War I.

1917 – Interstate bridge between Oregon and Washington opens.

1918 – First ship, the Kineo, launched by the Standifer Construction Company shipyard.

1925 – Army established Pearson Field.

1930s – Vancouver Barracks became district headquarters for the Ninth Corps of the Civilian Conservation Corps (CCC) under the command of General George C. Marshall.

1918 – Spruce Production Division under the direction of the U.S. Army Signal Corps was built, becoming the largest spruce mill in the country.

1918 – Armistace signed on November 11; Spruce Mill stopped production.

1918 – Spanish flu epidemic caused a city-wide shutdown.

1933 – Clark College established first institution of higher education in Southwest Washington.

1936-1938 – Regional CCC headquartered in Vancouver barracks under the command of General George C. Marshall.

1937 – First non-stop transpolar flight from Europe to America with a surprise landing at Pearson Air Field.

1940 – Alcoa Aluminum Plant begins production for the first aluminum to be manufactured in the West, continuing until 1986.

1942 – U.S. Army constructs emergency shipyard to meet production demands of U.S. Maritime Commission in World War II.

1942 – Kaiser Corporation builds shipyard at Ryan's Point on the Columbia, turning out more than 140 ships and two dry docks during WW II.

WW II – Vancouver Barracks serves as a training center and staging area for the Portland Subport of Embarkation.

1948 – Portions of barracks acreage transferred to the National Park Service (NPS) for the creation of Fort Vancouver as a National Historic Monument.

1987 – Officers Row transferred to the city.

1955 – Highway Interstate 5 opens in Vancouver on March 31.

1961 – Congress upgrades the designation of Fort Vancouver to National Historic Site and expands boundaries.

1970s – Federal dollars fund a National Park Service reconstruction of the old Hudson's Bay Company post.

1996 – Fort Vancouver National Site (officially the Vancouver National Historic Reserve) is formerly created by Congress as a 366-acre historic site.

1998 – Downtown renovation begins.

1998 – First annual Redheart Memorial begins at Fort Vancouver to honor the unjust imprisonment of Nez Perce in 1877-78.

2000 – Cowlitz tribe gets Federal Recognition which was reaffirmed in 2002.

2008 – West Barracks, including hospital and 1917 Red Cross building, are transferred to city.

2007 – Community leaders and developers purchase the former Boise Cascade mill site for redevelopment.

2012 – U.S. Army relinquishes ownership of their property at Fort Vancouver to the National Park Service.

2015 – **Providence Academy is** acquired by the Historic Trust, formerly called the Fort Vancouver Trust.

2016 – Vancouver Waterfront renovation begins.

2019 – Fort Vancouver NPS exceeds one million annual visitors.

2021 – Vancouver Riverwalk ranks number 13 as one of the best pedestrian attractions of its kind in the country by Fodor's Travel.

Firsts Monument

In 1925 the Washington State Society erected a memorial to commemorate a number of firsts that took place in Vancouver.
The first school
The first gospel sermon
The first marriage of American citizens
The first United States Military Post

Unfortunately one of the "firsts" that it acknowledged was listed as the "first civilization" which ignored the 15,000 years of Native American civilization long established in the area.

Perhaps in time a new firsts monument will be dedicated that is more accurate but for now this bit of slightly off listing "Vancouver Firsts" remains a historical landmark.

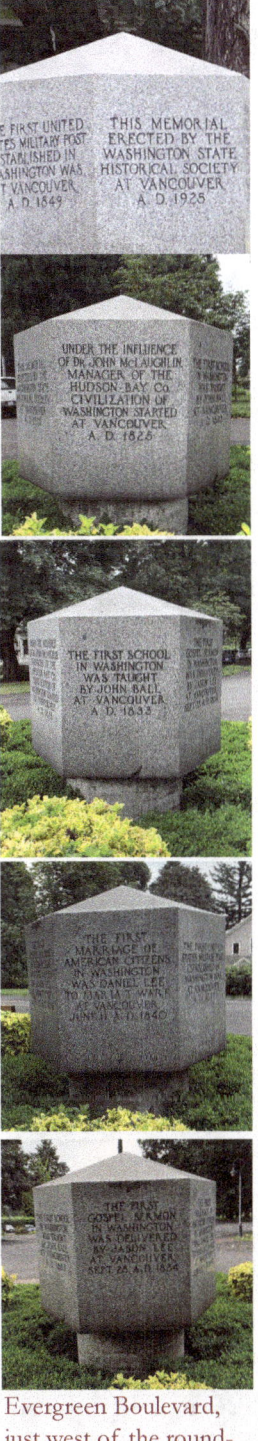

Evergreen Boulevard, just west of the roundabout on Officer's Row

Fort Vancouver
National HistoricSite

This historic site encompasses a reconstructed fort complete with vintage garden, fort walls, bastion, cannons, trade shop, and carpentry and blacksmith shops. Reenactors in historic dress cook over open hearths and hammer steel over forged fires, using simple, 19th-century tools. Carpenters using saws, hammers, and chisels create wood doors, furniture, and implements needed at the time for basic living and trade.

The best days to visit are Fridays and Saturdays, but you can take a self-guided tour anytime of the extensive grounds, including the Pearson Museum, Officers Quarters, the Barracks, and parade field. Stroll past the old mule barns where hundreds of mules were housed to use in the fort's earliest days to transport men and supplies from Alaska to California.

Pick up a free walking map and brochures at the Visitor Center, which also offers a short documentary about Fort Vancouver, the hub of the fur trade in the early 1880s. The Friends of the Fort Bookshop (where I work, by the way) is open Tuesday through Saturday. Stop in for souvenirs, unique and interpretive gifts relating to the site.

You can tour the fort for a fee, or take a self-guided walking tour using the app available on the website. Or simply follow the many historical markers along Officers Row, past Marshall House, the Pearson Museum, the Chkalov Monument, Spirit Pole, the First Japanese Memorial, a playground, picnicking spots, and walking trails.

1501 E Evergreen Blvd
Adult Fort Fee $10 (7-day pass)
nps.gov/fova/index.htm
360 816-6230

Visitor Center

A recommendation for getting the most out of your visit to Fort Vancouver and Vancouver Barracks is to start at the visitor center.

Tomas Villa's, Spirit Pole invites visitors to connect with Vancouver's earliest Native American history while a short introductory movie transports you through later historical mo-

ments from the Hudson Bay's Company to the first U.S. Army presence in the Pacific Northwest. Be sure to grab a walking map that will guide you along paved paths and roadways through the Vancouver Barracks, Fort Vancouver and Pearson Air Museum. Children are encouraged to draw and color fun moments of their visit to take home or display for others to enjoy.

Fort Bookstore & Gallery

This nonprofit store provides a wealth of Pacific Northwest information; Native American jewelry, crafts and artwork; books, maps, guides and even a selection of stuffies and toys that connect to life in the Pacific Northwest. Postcards, magnets, ornaments and other memorable keepsakes make this a nice stop for all things Fort Vancouver. Special events include author signings, workshops and presentations.

friendsfortvancouver.org *(Sign up for newsletter for events)*

Whose Anchor?

"This anchor was dredged from the Columbia River in 1960 near Fort Vancouver's wharf, one-quarter mile east of the Interstate 5 bridge. The anchor gives some answers about its history, but poses many more questions.

It is a Rogers Paten Small-Palm anchor, manufactured in England between 1815 and 1850. The chain is wrought iron stud, used by the British Navy, and probably others, beginning in 1808. This size of anchor came from a ship of 1,000 tons or more, a large ship of the period.

Records of which ship lost this important equipment have not been found. So we are left to speculate about its origins. Is the anchor from a commercial ship visiting Fort Vancouver between 1825 and 1850? The Hudson's Bay Company had many ships in service on the Pacific Coast transporting agricultural goods, salmon, lumber, and furs to Russian Alaska, Hawaii, and England.

Perhaps ths anchor is from a war ship? Before the current border between the United States and Canada was established in 1846, England and the United States had naval ships in the Northwest protecting their conflicting interests. Is the anchor naval or commercial, what do you think?"

E Evergreen Way on the left of the Visitor Center.

Text from NPS interpretative panel at Fort Vancouver NPS

First Japanese in North America

English translation

"In October 1832, the Japanese cargo ship Hojun Maru set sail from near Nagoya bound for Edo (present day Tokyo).

Disabled in a storm off Enshu Nada, the Hojun Maru drifted for fourteen months before running aground on the coast near Cape Flattery, at the northwest tip of what is now Washington State. The three surviving crew members, Iwakichi, Otokichi and Kyukichi lived briefly among the coastal tribes before they were brought here to Fort Vancouver by the Hudson's Bay Company.

They were the first Japanese to arrive on the continent of North America. ..."

E Evergreen Way on the right of the Visitor Center

See Sakura Festival at Clark College - page 35

Hudson's Bay Company Fort

FUR TRADE CAPITAL OF THE PACIFIC COAST

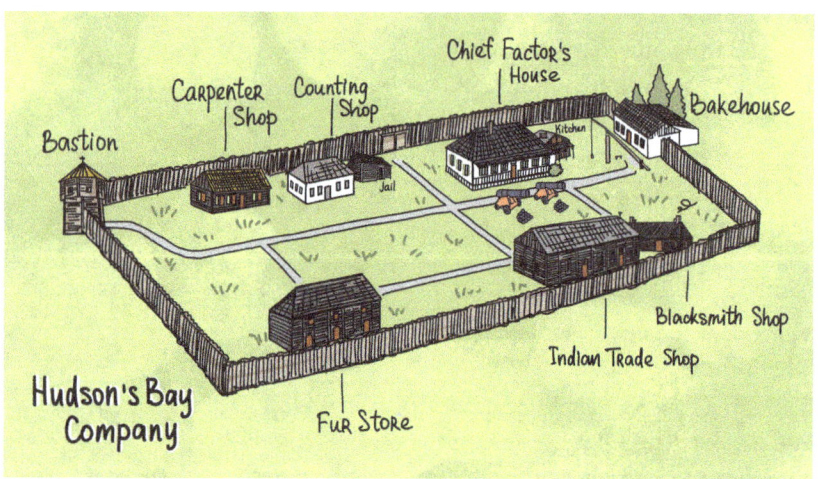

Welcome to Fort Vancouver

The London-based Hudson's Bay Company established an extensive fur trading network throughout the Pacific Northwest, utilizing two dozen posts, six ships, and about 600 employees during peak seasons.

Fort Vancouver was the administrative center and principal supply depot of the "Columbia Department," controlling 700,000 square miles stretching from Russian Alaska to Mexican California, and from the Rocky Mountains to the Pacific Ocean.

The fort became a center of activity and influence, supported by a multicultural village with inhabitants from over 35 different ethnic and tribal groups. The first hospital, school, library, grist mill, saw mill, dairy, shipbuilding, and orchard in the region were all centered at Fort Vancouver.

A part of the National Park System since 1948, today the park is also part of the Vancouver National Historic Reserve.

Fort Vancouver has been designated the premier historical archaeological site in the Pacific Northwest. A strong combination of archaeological and historical informs the way the site is reconstructed and its past shared with visitors.

A collection of over two million museum items is cared for here, spanning the American Indian, fur trade, and U.S. Army occupations of the area.

Text from NPS interpretative panel at Fort Vancouver NPS

An English Garden

Planting a garden was one of the first things the Hudson's Bay Company (HBC) did when they established Fort Vancouver. At its height, in the mid-1840s, the garden had expanded to eight acres and provided not only produce but also large numbers of flowering plants, shrubs, and fruit trees for the pleasure of the fort's residents and visitors. This large gardening operation was symbolic of the power that the HBC exerted over the entire region and was representative of their extensive agricultural enterprises.

In 1836, American missionary Henry Spalding described the garden as"…about 5 acres laid out in good order, stored with almost every species of vegetables, fruit trees, and flowers." His observations of the region's farming potential, and those of other Americans, stimulated immigration from the eastern United States. In 1843 approximately 900 settlers made the journey to Fort Vancouver. By 1846 more than 8,000 settlers had arrived in the Oregon Country, leading to the end of HBC dominance.

The garden today is a small, interpretive representation of the larger historic garden. A dedicated cadre of volunteers and staff plant heirloom fruits, vegetables, herbs, and flowers to give a feeling for the abundance that was once here. Just as in the 1840s, the plants found in today's garden provide produce for the fort's kitchen and a place of beauty and rest for visitors.

The fort's original orchard was characterized by full size, ungrafted apple trees with wide spacing. Today, this style of "farm orchard" has been recreated with seedlings of old English cider varieties and clones of Vancouver's Old Apple Tree. Modern rendition, courtesy of the National Park Service.

Text from NPS interpretative panel at Fort Vancouver NPS

The fort had a single **bastion** built into a corner wall of the fort.

It held **cannons** that were mostly used for ceremonial purposes to welcome ships and trading vessels with an official greeting.

The **carpenter shop** was in constant demand for doors, window casings, furniture, wagons and the planning of other buildings.

Today expert carpenters in period dress using only the tools and expertise of the time continue to make everything from tables, benches, doors and floors to wheelbarrows and 18th century toys.

A minimum of four **black-smiths** employed at a time were kept busy making tools like hammers, nails, axes, knives and even saw blades. They also made building items such as doorknobs, locks, hinges and window fasteners to kitchen implements such as pots and kettles to cooking spoons and hooks to hang things on.

Men and women ate separately but elegantly at the Factor House.

Meals for the Chief Factor, officers, family and guests were prepared in a separate kitchen located next to the Factor house.

Separate from the cookhouse was the bakehouse used for baking bread and mountains of sea biscuits that would be used for sailors, trapping brigades, other forts and for commercial sale.

Animal pelts, primarily beaver brought to the fort were kept in "stores", or warehouses. The furs were inventoried, cleaned, and pressed into bales before being shipped. In 1843, more than 61,000 furs were sent to England with each beaver pelt valued at about $170 of today's value. The fur trade was a profitable business.

The Indian trade shop was a busy place for purchases of all kinds.

The Vancouver Farm

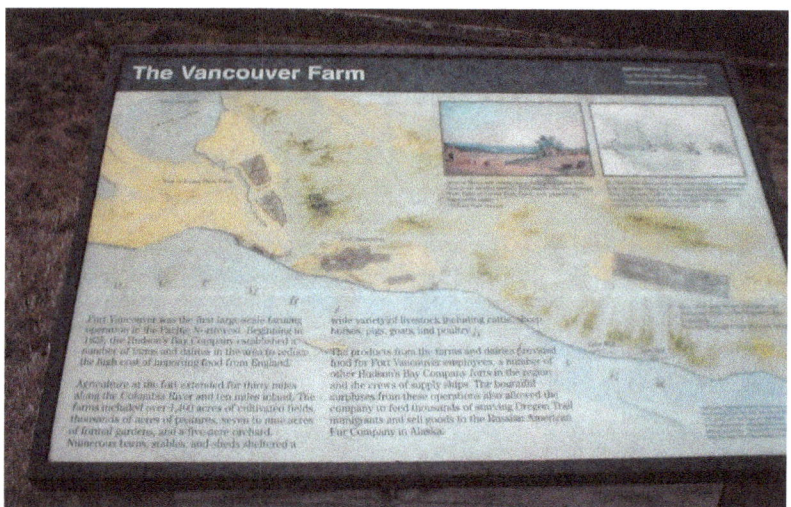

Fort Vancouver was the first large-scale farming operation in the Pacific Northwest. Beginning in 1825, the Hudson's Bay Company established a number of farms and dairies in the area to reduce the high cost of importing food from England.

Agriculture at the fort extended for thirty miles along the Columbia River and ten miles inland. The farms included over 1,400 acres of cultivated fields, thousands of acres of pastures, seven to nine acres of formal gardens, and a five-acre orchard.

Numerous barns, stables, and sheds sheltered a wide variety of livestock including cattle, sheep, horses, pigs, goats, and poultry.

The products from the farms and dairies provided food for Fort Vancouver employees, a number of other Hudson's Bay Company forts in the region and crews of supply ships. The bountiful surpluses from these operations also allowed the company to feed thousands of starving Oregon Trail immigrants and sell goods to the Russian American Fur Company in Alaska.

Many **heritage seeds** are harvested each year from the Fort Garden and are available for sale in the Friends Bookstore.

Vegetables: Tomatoes, lettuce, beans, etc.

Flowers: Cardoon, poppies, marigolds, zinnias and more.

All proceeds from the store go to support Fort Activities and transportation aid for local school bus tours.

U.S Army Arrived

The U. S. Army arrived in the Pacific Northwest in 1949 in response to the Whitman massacre and other Indian uprisings. The soldiers arrived at Vancouver, first by ship. A few months later, overland reinforcements arrived with 1,000 men, 700 horses, 1,200 mules, and 171 supply wagons.

Vancouver Barracks was the headquarters for the military's response to conflicts in Alaska, Washington, Idaho, and parts of Montana, and it sent out personal and goods for many conflicts from the Spanish American War through World War II.

The number of soldiers stationed here rose and fell according to need. During World War I, it swelled to 30,000 with the Spruce Production Squadron, and then it dwindled after the war. It was made the Pacific Northwest Headquarters for the Civilian Conservation Corps (CCC) until WW II.

Vancouver Barracks was responsible for the Kaiser Shipyards, established in 1942 with 38,000 workers operating around the clock to produce 10 Liberty ships, 30 landing craft, 50 escort aircraft carriers, 31 attack transports, 12 C-4 troopships, 8 C-4 cargo vessels, and 2 (14,000-ton) dry docks.

After WW II, the military presence dwindled, ending completely in 2011. Today, many streets and landmarks provide lasting significance of the U.S. Army's 160-year-plus presence in Clark County.

Vancouver Barracks Plan

A MODEL FOR HISTORIC SITE REUSE

The 33 acres and 20 historic buildings in the eastern and southern portions of Vancouver Barracks are now part of Fort Vancouver National Historic Site, your national park.

A Master Plan for the site was developed with input from the public, our partners, and agency specialists.

It provides a compelling vision for what this site will become over the next few years, merging the National Park Service mission with the goals of the community.

While preserving the historic character of the buildings, the archaeological resources underground, and the cultural landscape, the NPS and its many partners will bring Vancouver Barracks into its next chapter of public service.

Public agencies, nonprofits, and community groups, retail and commercial businesses will come together to transform this former military post into a vibrant, accessible campus.

It will take time to achieve the entire vision laid out in the Master Plan, but this site will move steadily towards its new role as a model for the responsible reuse of historic sites. Many exciting changes are on the horizon!

Text from NPS interpretative panel at Fort Vancouver NPS

Parade Ground & Bandstand

Social events, such as parades, dances, and concerts, helped establish and maintain positive public relations between the nineteenth century U.S. Army and neighboring communities.

At Vancouver Barracks, military bands often served as local ambassadors, providing free public concerts in local cities and at the post. During summer months, many of the post's concerts and social events centered around the bandstand.

Through historical and archaeological evidence, we know of the presence of three bandstands at the post.

The first appears on maps from 1870. It was constructed on the parade ground south of the Grant House, slightly to the east of the current bandstand.

By the mid-1880s it had been replaced by a fountain, and the second bandstand had been constructed on the extreme west end of the parade ground.

It, in turn, was supplanted by a third bandstand built around 1906 on the east end of the parade ground, which stood until 1943.

The current bandstand is a reconstruction built in the 1980s, meant to duplicate the post's first bandstand.

Like its predecessors, it serves as the social center of the site, hosting speeches, ceremonies, weddings, commemorations, and – continuing the rich legacy of the site – military concerts.

Text from NPS interpretative panel at Fort Vancouver NPS

"Soldiers and civilians alike enjoyed garrison concerts, winter lectures, parades, and Fourth of July celebrations"

VNHRHistory PartOne1846-1898 pdf

East Barracks

The National Park System is responsible for the area known as the Western Barracks and the City of Vancouver (maintained by the Historic Trust) cares for the Eastern Barracks. Currently none of the buildings are open to the public but markers and information panels offer a self-guided tour through the first and for many years the most important military installation in the Pacific Northwest.

Double Infantry Barracks **1** (#982), **2** (#989) & **4** (#993)
3 Post Headquarters (#991)
5 (#704) Barber Shop
6 (#725) JAG
7 (#722) Mess Hall
8 (#721) Auditorium
9 (#746) Band Training Building
10 (#748) Motor Shop Building
11 (#728) Finance Office
12 (#733) Mess Hall
13 (#754) AFFEES
14 (#786) Wood Shop
15 (#753) Storage.
16 (#752) Quartermaster Storehouse

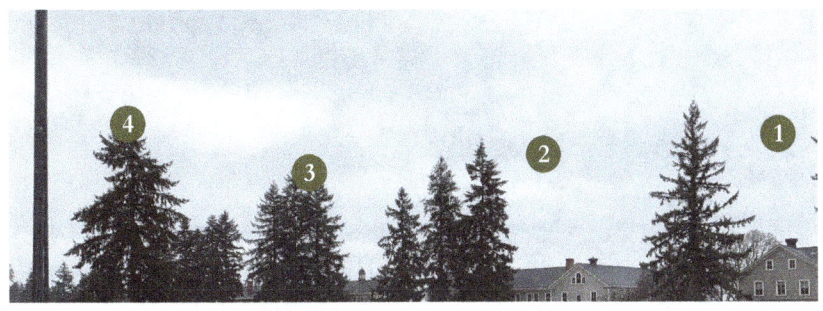

Double Infantry Barracks

Front and back view of the barracks are quite different. In the beginning I often thought I was looking at two sets of buildings.

1. **Barracks** - Building 987 built in **1906**
2. **Barracks** Building 989 built in **1904**
4. **Barracks** Building 993 built in **1906**

Typically these barracks held 180 soldiers and NCO officers.

The Post Headquarters built in **1906.**

Clark County Veterans Monument Dedicated [1998] to those who died in defense of our Country in the Spanish-American War, World Wars I and II.

704 Barber shop then office building 1934. Barbers in the military at this time could be either civilian or military. The Barracks employed many civilians during the 164 years in Vancouver providing jobs and an economic boost to the area.

725 JAG (Judge Advocate General) building. Mandated with the mission of defending the Army and its Soldiers in all military legal matters. At one time was also the Post Exchange with a restaurant.

722 [1914] This small building next to the Gymnasium served as a Mess Hall and later as an Army Reserve Recruitment Office.

723 Auditorium (Gymnasium) [1904-1905]. Front view. It was important for morale to provide recreation for the soldiers. It also helped to lower work for the JAG folks defending the mischief and disorderly conduct soldiers might get into off base.

746 [1905] Workshops - 104th [1940] Division Band Training Building. Military bands played an important role both for soldiers and as social ambassadors in local communities. Free public concerts at the Fort Bandstand were widely attended.

748 Motor Repair Shop 1918-1919. The Motor Transport Corps (MTC) was formed in August 1918 and it did not take long for Vancouver Barracks to step up with its own first motor repair shop.

#728 built in 1941 as a **Finance Office**. In 1941 the post was at its height with billets for 250 officers and over 7000 soldiers in transit for WWII assignments. Today the building is used as headquarters for the Bureau of Indian Affairs.

#733 built in 1919 as a Mess Hall. Vancouver Barracks in 1919 was a World War I demobilization center with 30,000 leaving the army from here. In 1920 only a small presence of Company B, 32nd Infantry remained until the next armed conflict.

754 Quartermaster Shop now the AFEES (Army & Air Force Exchange Service). The first PX in the military began at Vancouver Barracks as a way to keep soldiers entertained

786 Workshop built in 1905-1906. Later used as Wood Shop and Red Cross. Soldiers carry out many roles of service that do not involve actual fighting or keeping peace. Today there are over 10,000 different occupational specialties in the military.

753 [1917] Small building built for storage. At one time the barracks consisted of as many as 300 buildings many of which were moved or torn down making way for other functions as needed.

752 [1905] Quartermaster Storehouse - one time Postal Exchange. The quartermaster was the officer in charge of supply support for soldiers. Ulysses S. Grant was the quartermaster during his time at Vancouver Barracks.

West Barracks

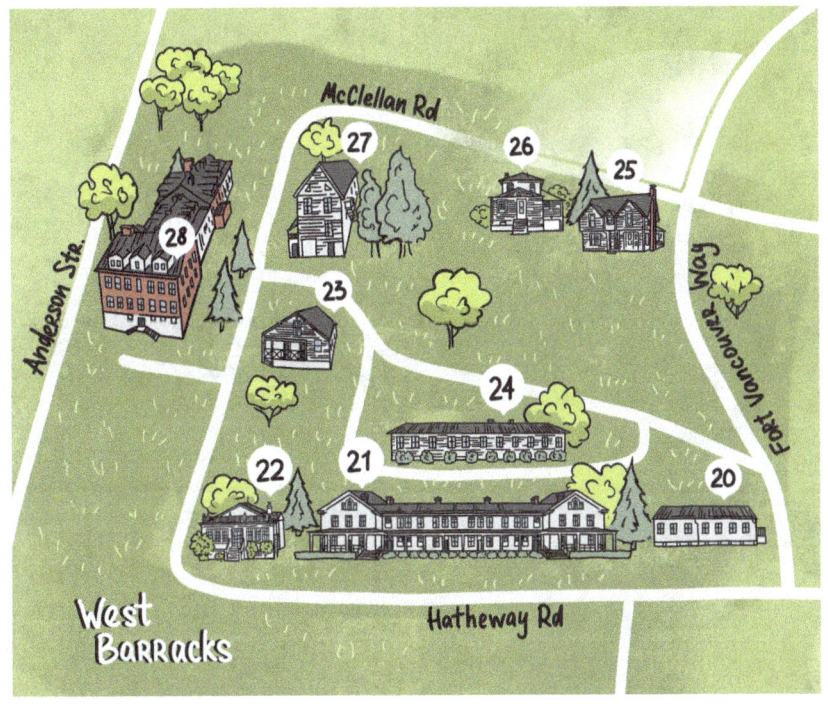

20 Building 630 Quartermaster (Spruce Division Records Storehouse #630)
21 Building 638 Artillery Barracks
22 Building 636 Red Cross Building
23 Building 626 Dental Surgery
24 Building 628 Mess Hall
25 Building 631 Hospital Sergeants Quarters
26 Building 621 Hospital Steward's Quarters
27 Building 607 Infantry Barracks
28 Building 614 Post Hospital

Not pictured on map
O O Howard House
Old Mule Barn
NCO Family Quarters (located on South side of Hatheway Road in front of Double Artillery Barracks.
   H1, H2, H3, H4, H5

O. O. Howard House

This Italianate-Revival style home was built in 1878 for General Oliver Otis Howard, Commanding General of the Department of the Columbia from 1874 until 1880.

This gracious home was considered "the finest dwelling house north of the Columbia." It was home to many social events and hosted several famous guests, including Ulysses S. Grant in 1879 and U.S. President Rutherford B. Hayes in 1880.

After the Marshall House was built as the new department commander's home in 1886, the Howard House became the local post commander's residence. It then served as a Non-Commissioned Officers' (NCO) Club from 1934 until it was surplused after a fire in 1986.

Notable Civil War General Howard was lauded for his work with African Americans when he was Commissioner of the Freedman's Bureau from 1866 until 1872, and for helping to found Howard University, an all African American institution.

However, Howard's reputation for his role in the Indian Wars campaigns against Native American groups resisting pressure to move to reservations was not as positive.

The most famous of these campaigns was the 1877 Nez Perce War, in which Chief Joseph led his people in an unprecedented five-month flight from northeastern Oregon to Montana, until their capture by Howard and his soldiers. Howard also unjustly incarcerated Nez Perce Chief Temme Ilppilp (Red Heart) and thirty-two of his people at Fort Vancouver for eight months in 1877.

General Oliver Otis Howard, Commander of the Department of the Columbia, 1874-1880.
National Archives and Records Administration

Text from NPS interpretative panel at Fort Vancouver NPS

#20 Building 630 built in **[1906]** as a Mess Hall then in 1936 changed to Storehouse for Spruce Production Corporation records. After 1953 it was altered to 10 rooms and hallway and used as **Quartermaster's Storehouse**.

#21 Building 638 built in **[1904]** a **Double Artillery Barracks** to house 240 soldiers *(see page 79).*

#22 Building 636 [1918-1919] Red Cross Convalescent House. Built originally for patient care and morale it transitioned in 1921 to the Army and became a Non-Commissioned Officers' Club offering movies, parties, and dances. *(see page 75).*

#23 Building 626 [1956] The building was created from an older building [1888] which was the dead house (mortuary). Later in 1910 it became the hospital tool shed. In 1956 it was remodeled to become the **Dental Surgeon's Office and Dental Clinic**.

#24 Building 628 [1914] Mess Hall with kitchen. In 1930 it was equipped with one coal range, one range boiler, one refrigerator, and one kitchen sink.

#25 Building 631 [1887-1888]
Hospital Steward's Quarters then renamed in 1934 to Hospital Sergeant's Quarters. The Steward's role functioned as the hospital administrator, pharmacist, and director of male nurses.

#26 Building 621 [1905 & 1908]
Hospital Sergeant's Quarters. As administrator of the hospital it was important that the Sergeant would be close at hand for emergencies and hospital decisions that needed to be handled immediately.

#27 Building 607 [1887]
   The oldest barracks at Vancouver Barracks was built to house 48 men of the 14th Infantry.
   It functioned as a complete unit consisting of offices, store rooms, dining room, kitchen and dormitory.

#29 Building 628 [1910]
Old Mule Barn built for 134 horses and mules. Mules were used to carry supplies, rations, sundries and ammunition. A four pack of mules hitched together carried artillery gun pieces such as a Vickers gun (machine gun) and ammunition.

Double Artillery Barracks

At the beginning of the 20th century, Vancouver was the headquarters for the Department of the Columbia, a vast administrative unit in the Northwest.

The population of the post almost tripled in response to increased military activity both at home and abroad.

There were not enough barracks for soldiers stationed here, and men were sleeping in tents. An ambitious building scheme was begun that would enable the post to garrison a regiment of infantry and two batteries of artillery. The double artillery barracks was constructed during that period, erected on this site in 1904.

The Colonial Revival style building house two separate companies, a total capacity of 240 men.

The latrines, storage rooms, and other functional spaces were located in the basement. The kitchen, mess halls, and day rooms were on the first floor.

The second floor had large dormitory style sleeping quarters for the soldiers, with smaller, semi-private rooms for the officers. At one point, the attic housed an indoor shooting range.

The Barracks housed troops like the "Mountain Battery of The 4th Field Artillery, seen here on the parade ground next to the O. O. Howard House.

Text from NPS interpretative panel at Fort Vancouver NPS

Post Hospital

#28 Building 614 [1904]

This Post Hospital at its time was considered one of the best military hospitals in the nation caring for wounded soldiers, sick and injured lumber workers and influenza victims. It was active through the 1940s.

Elements of the hospital from floor plan of 1903 building report.

First Floor Main Building

Surgeon's Office
Assistant Surgeon's Office
Dispensary
Hospital Steward's Office
Dental Surgery
Wardmaster
Examination Room
First Floor Annex
Dining Room
Kitchen
Special Diet Kitchen
Pantries (2)

Second Floor Main Building

Officers' Ward
Laboratory
Operating Room
Etherizing Room
Surgical ward
Acting Hospital Steward's Office
Second Floor Annex
Dormitories
Isolation Ward
Prison Ward

Third Floor Main Building

XRayRoom

Red Cross Convalescent Center

Following the nation's entry into World War I, the American Red Cross was authorized to construct convalescent houses adjacent to military hospitals.

These facilities provided recreation away from a hospital atmosphere, and helped boost the morale of recuperating patients. The Red Cross provided writing supplies, books, games, movies, and other diversions, and offered hospitality to visiting family members.

The construction of this building, a unique adaptation to standard plans, was completed in only four months due to the efforts of local trade unions and widespread community support.

The convalescent house at Vancouver Barracks was dedicated in February of 1919, and for a time continued its role in patient care.

It was furnished with locally-made wicker furniture and the flags of World War I allies.

The last hostess for the convalescent house was E. B. Hamilton, after whom the main hall is now named.

As the activities of the Red Cross diminished, the building was transferred to the Army and became a Non-Commissioned Officers' Club offering a variety of recreational activities, including movies, parties, and dances.

Text from NPS interpretative panel at Fort Vancouver NPS

The Red Cross
women tended
to the soldiers
at Vancouver Barracks

*VNHRHistory
PartTwo1898-1920 pdf*

Pearson Air Museum

The 321st Observation Squadron (1923-1941)

"Although the U.S. Army allowed civilian aircraft to land at Vancouver Barracks beginning in 1905, military aircraft began operating here in 1921, when the U.S. Army Air Service established a landing field for an aviation forest patrol. The patrol was a cooperative forest fire spotting effort by the U.S. Army and the U.S. Forest Service. Two years later, the 321st Observation Squadron arrived at Vancouver Barracks, with three biplanes initially stationed at the field. ..."

"Pearson Field is the first airport in the Pacific Northwest and one of the oldest operating airports in the United States. ..."

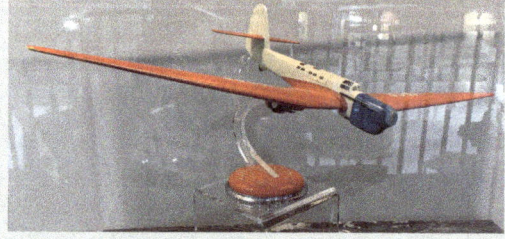

Soviet Transpolar Flight of 1937

Excerpt: "Near this site at Pearson Airfield on June 20th, 1937, three Soviet aviators completed the first non-stop flight from the U.S.S.R. to the U.S.A.

Text from NPS interpretative panels at Fort Vancouver NPS

Who was
Pearson?

Lieutenant Alexander Pearson Jr. was a renowned test pilot in the early US Army Air Service and a daring stunt flyer. Pearson was born and raised in Kansas, but his family moved to Portland, Oregon, after he joined the service, and he attended the University of Oregon in Eugene. In 1924, he tragically died in a plane crash at the age of 28 while test flying a US Navy airplane at a speed in excess of 200 mph.

The public adored and respected Pearson, and his premature death caused an outpouring of affection. On April 4, 1925, the Secretary of War ordered that the landing field at Vancouver Barracks be renamed Pearson Field in honor of this brave pilot.

Continue through the exhibits and explore the fascinating history of early aviation at Pearson Field!

Welcome to
Pearson
Air Museum!

Today, more than eight million people fly on airplanes every single day. Airplanes are used for travel, mail and package delivery, military purposes, and to monitor and survey the Earth from above. Can you imagine what life was like before airplanes? Just think about how exhilarating and terrifying it must have been to fly one of the first planes.

Ever since the dawn of modern flight in the early 1900s, Pearson Field has been a gathering place for airplane enthusiasts, visionaries, and experimenters.

Pearson Field is one of the oldest, continually operated airfields in the United States.

More than a century ago, trans](ns risked their lives to make air travel a safe and reliable form of transportation. Find out how this site was home to the earliest pilots in the region, became the biggest lumber mill in the world, and has been serving military and civilian interests ever since. By looking to the past, we can understand how today's aviation industry and how these early years shaped the world we know today.

We invite you to read some of the experimental aviators and experience the dramatic adventures that put Pearson Field on the map.

Less than two years after the Wright brothers made history, a small field at Vancouver Barracks became an airfield.

Six years later, the U. S. Army declared the field an "Aviation Camp" and, in 1912, it was the scene for the first airmail flight sanctioned by the U. S. Post Office and the first interstate flight between Washington and Oregon.

On April 6, 1917, the United States entered into World War I, and soon work began just west of Pearson Field to build the world's largest spruce-milling operation, producing enough lumber for 300 airplanes.

By 1923, the airfield had become recognized as a major airport and U. S. Army Air Base, playing a key role in the development of U.S. air power and general aviation in the Pacific Northwest.

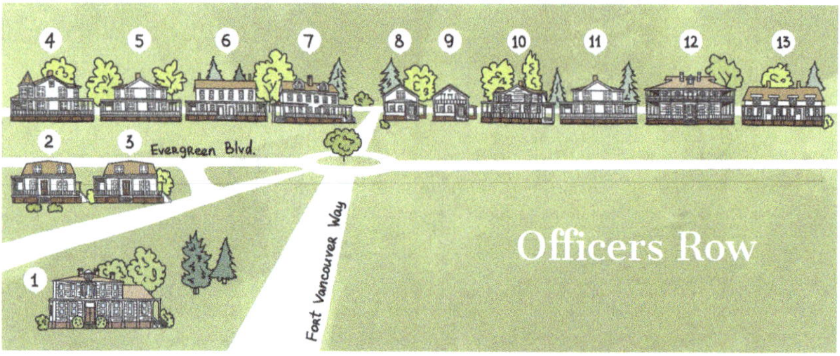

1101 Officers Row

12

GRANT HOUSE The first officer house built in **1849**, constructed of hard hewn logs was for the commanding officer. Other log structures were built quickly following this for other officers but none of these remain. In those first years the houses were rough log buildings built with green wood. As the wood dried space between the logs expanded leaving large cracks so there was little protection from cold, damp weather. In those early years there was so much work to be done in establishing the base that comfort even for officers was low in priority.

901,03,05 Officers Row

951,53,55 Officers Row

Twelve years would pass before two more houses were built for officers in **1867**. These two homes seem less elegant compared to the other houses we see in the Row but in the time they were built they were prized dwellings with tall ceilings, fireplaces, glass windows and many other comfort amenities.

750 Anderson St A

It would be eleven more years in **1878** when another grand building was added which would function as a command center and an officer home. General O. O. Howard as Commander of the Department of the Columbia stayed here with his family till 1881 when Gen. Nelson A Miles took over command and moved in with his family until 1885.

800,02,04,06 Officers Row

Built in **1881** this large home would house more than one officer family. The molded doors have octagonal panels associated with the Italianate style. This feature is not found on any of the other buildings on the Row.

Marshall House

MARSHALL HOUSE:
Open to the Public
This house is the only Queen Anne style home on the row. At the second level, the tiny window in the turret is beveled.

The house is named for Gen. George C. Marshall, author of the Marshall Plan for the economic rebuilding of Europe and Japan following World War II, Secretary of State and recipient of the Nobel Peace Prize.

Gen. Marshall served as Commander of the Department of the Columbia and lived in this house from 1936-7.

A Look Down Officers Row

The largest collection of historically restored officer housing in the country resides along Evergreen Blvd, a tree-lined street known as Officers Row.

Twenty-one homes built between 1850 and 1906 housed commanding officers of the U. S. Army through numerous conflicts starting with the Indian Wars up to and through World War II.

Each home has its own history, but the three most prestigious are the Grant House, Marshall House, and O. O. Howard House. Other homes occupied by lower ranking officers later played major roles in the U. S. Army to the point that over 70 of the officers who were stationed here later became prominent generals in various conflicts.

The Marshall House, in Queen Anne style, is presently the only home open to the public, and that is limited to the first floor. The tour is free, and it provides an inside look at an elite Army Officer residence of the 19th century.

Historical markers and information panels along Officers Row share important dates and events of the military presence in Vancouver beginning in 1849.

House **#18** built in **1885** and the next three built in **1886** were styled much the same except for the doors. Because of their distinctive form locals began calling them the "Officers Row style" homes.

1401,03-07 Officers Row

1451,53-57 Officers Row

1051,53-59 Officers Row

1501,03-07 Officers Row

1351,53 Officers Row

This long, low multi-dwelling follows the tradition of the south with four, delicate multi-light doors that open out to the verandah.

1551,53-67 Officers Row

1001,03-09 Officers Row

601 Officers Row

701 Officers Row

Vancouver Business Journal

These three almost identical houses exhibit the roof form known as a mansard, typical of Second Empire architecture.

These two houses built on either side of the Grant House offer a new feature: the corner turret capping a full-height rectangular bay window. The bellcast form of this turret is referred to as a witch's hat.

750,52-56 Officers Row

Built in 1886-87. Exhibiting influence from the Queen Anne style, these buildings have a full-height rectangular bay window capped by a truncated, bellcast, hip roof with paired windows.

1101 Officers Row

Officers Row

1001,03-09 Officers Row

Built in **1886-87**. This simple-gable roofed building is punctuated by shed-roof wall dormers. A wall dormer differs from other dormers in that the dormer is a continuation, or extension of the façade wall. Notice that the width of the front doors is greater than the others on the row.

1151,53-67 Officers Row

Built in **1903**. This building has many classically-inspired features including the formal façade and the Palladian-esque window at the attic level. The window has a central arched component flanked by two rectangular components, a definitive characteristic of the Palladian style.

1601,03-07 Officers Row

Built in **1906-7**. The last building built on the Row. Colonial Revival architecture, with columns recalling ancient Greek temples. Triangular shapes are one of the easiest clues to identifying classically-inspired styles. Note the triangles outlined by the trim boards on the side walls and dormers.

Columbia Land Trust - Officers Row

Interesting note is that the Covington House (oldest home in Clark County - page 19) was built in **1848** (possibly much earlier). Ulysses S. Grant when he was a quartermaster at the fort from 1852-1853 would often go there for an evening entertainment. The Covington House will give you an idea of log cabin construction in that time period. If you visit note the huge amount of chinking between logs (easily two to three inches) and you will get an idea how cold those first officer houses were without proper chinking.

Officers Row – Historic Markers

Historic Markers placed before each of the homes on Officers Row provide a snapshot of important events that took place during the U. S. Army's 160 years (1849-2012) in Vancouver. A few are included here.

Information panels provide additional historic facts making a visit to Officers Row a power packed walkthrough of early U. S. Army history in the Pacific Northwest.

UNITED STATES MILITARY HEROES DATES OF SERVICE IN VANCOUVER

Rufus Ingalls	1849-53
E. O. C. Ord	1850's
William Wing Loring	1850-51
Ulysses S. Grant	1852-54
B. L. E. Bonneville	1853-55
Philip H. Sheridan	1856
William S. Harney	1858-59
O. O. Howard	1874-81
Geoge Goethals	1880's
Nelson Miles	1881-86
Thomas Anderson	1886-98
John Gibbon	1886
George C. Marshall	1936-38

Donated by First Independent Bank

FAMOUS VISITORS TO OFFICERS' ROW

General Ambrose Burnside
Mrs. George Armstrong Custer
Jefferson C. Davis
President Rutherford B. Hayes
Walla Walla Chief Homily
Nez Perce Chief Joseph
General H. A. Morrow
Methow Chief Moses
George Pickett
President Franklin Delano Roosevelt
General Winfield Scott
Moses Williams

Donated by Byron W. Lin and Aron Jacobus and family

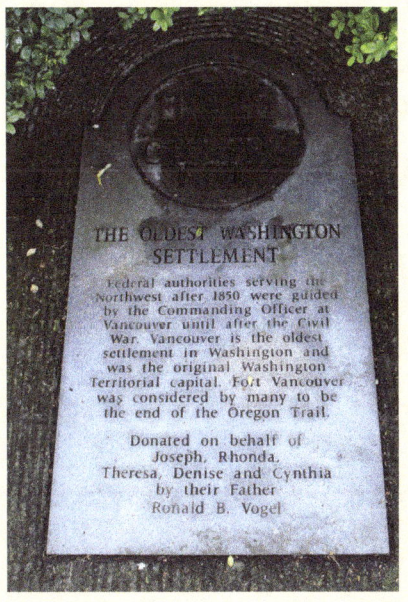

Oldest Washington Settlement

Federal authorities serving the Northwest after 1850 were guided by the Commanding Officer at Vancouver until after the Civil War.

Vancouver is the oldest settlement in Washington and was the original Washington Territorial capital.

Fort Vancouver was considered by many to be the end of the Oregon Trail.

Donated on behalf of Joseph, Rhonda, Theresa, Denise and Cynthia by their Father Ronald B. Vogel

The Great Explorations

A stake in front of the Grant house once marked the spot where, in 1853, Captain George B. McClellan set out to find routes through the Cascade Mountains for the Pacific Railroad.

Under the direction of General Nelson A. Miles in the 1880's expeditions were sent to trace the Yukon and Putnam Rivers in Alaska.

George Goethals, later chief engineer for the Panama Canal, received his first major assignment at Vancouver to explore the territory between Old Fort Colville and Lake Osoyoos on the Canadian Border.

Donated by Pacific Telecom Inc.

Texts of interpretive markers for Officers Row

National Registered Sites

Slocum House

There are over 50 historic sites throughout Vancouver and many more throughout Clark County. While many of them are not open to the public on a daily basis one can visit the city's web page for the site or drive by to step back for a glimpse of Vancouver's past.

Entries listed by location

Vancouver

Wisteria Court Apartments
2218 Broadway St [c. 1929]
clark.wa.gov/community-planning/
wisteria-court-apartments

Vancouver Main Post Office
1211 Daniels St   [c. 1917]
clark.wa.gov/community-planning/
vancouver-main-post-office

Slocum House
605 Esther St [c. 1867]
clark.wa.gov/community-planning/
slocum-house

Lloyd DuBois House
902 Esther St [c. 1902]
clark.wa.gov/community-planning/
lloyd-dubois-house

Langsdorf House
1010 Esther St [c. 1910]
clark.wa.gov/community-planning/
langsdorf-house

Charles Zimmerman House
1812 Columbia St [c. 1906]
clark.wa.gov/community-planning/
charles-zimmerman-house

Steffan House
2000 Columbia St [c. 1909]
clark.wa.gov/community-planning/
steffan-house

Clark County Courthouse
1200 Franklin St [1941]
clark.wa.gov/superior-court

John P. and Mary Kiggins House
2404 H St [1907]
clark.wa.gov/community-planning/
john-p-and-mary-kiggins-house

Bailey-Dickerson House
2613 H St [1905]
clark.wa.gov/community-planning/
bailey-dickerson-house

Evergreen Hotel
500 Main St [c. 1928]
clark.wa.gov/community-planning/
evergreen-hotel

Vancouver National Bank Building
518 Main St [c. 1906]
clark.wa.gov/community-planning/
vancouver-national-bank-building

US National Bank Building
601 Main St [c. 1912]

Sparks Engleman Building
605-607 Main St [1903]
clark.wa.gov/community-planning/
sparks-engleman-building

Melvin's Men's Shop
901 Main St [1934]
clark.wa.gov/community-planning/
melvins-mens-shop

Kiggins 1922 Building
904 Main St [1922]
clark.wa.gov/community-planning/
kiggins-1922-building

Elks Building
916 Main St [c. 1911]
clark.wa.gov/community-planning/
elks-building

Kiggins Theater
1011 Main St [1936]
kigginstheatre.com/now-playing
clark.wa.gov/community-planning/
kiggins-theater

Vancouver Federal Savings Loan
1001 Main St [1929]
clark.wa.gov/community-planning/
vancouver-federal-savings-and-loan-
building

Carnegie Library
1511 Main St [c. 1909]
clark.wa.gov/community-planning/
carnegie-library

Covington House
4201 Main St [1846]
covingtonhistorichouse.com

Fort Vancouver
612 E Reserve St [c. 1824]
Reconstruction began in 1966.
nps.gov/fova/index.htm

Pearson Field
E Reserve St and E. 5th St
[c. 1905-1941]
nps.gov/fova/learn/historyculture/
pearson.htm

DuBois Motors Company Building
500 Washington St [1927-1928]
clark.wa.gov/community-planning/
dubois-motors-company-building

Sedgwick Building
801 Washington St [1907]
clark.wa.gov/community-planning/
sedgwick-building

Ranck Building
901 Washington St [1908]
clark.wa.gov/community-planning/
ranck-building

Greely Building
1012 Washington St [c. 1920]
clark.wa.gov/community-planning/
greely-building

Luepke Florist
1300 Washington St [1937/1945]
clark.wa.gov/community-planning/
luepke-florist

Lucky Lager Warehouse
215 W. 4th St [c. 1920]
clark.wa.gov/community-planning/
lucky-lager-warehouse

Chumasero-Smith House
310 W. 11th St [c. 1903]
clark.wa.gov/community-planning/
chumasero-smith-house

Kettenring House
314 W. 11th St [c. 1908]
clark.wa.gov/community-planning/
kettenring-house

Vancouver Telephone Exchange
112 W. 11th St [c. 1934]
clark.wa.gov/community-planning/
vancouver-telephone-exchange

Melvin's Men's Shop
901 Main St [1934]
clark.wa.gov/community-planning/
melvins-mens-shop

St. James Catholic Church
204 W. 12th St [c. 1885]
clark.wa.gov/community-planning/
st-james-catholic-church

Lowell M. Hidden House
100 W. 13th St [c.1885]
clark.wa.gov/community-planning/
lowell-m-hidden-house

W. Foster Hidden House
110 W. 13th St [c. 1913]
clark.wa.gov/community-
planning/w-foster-hidden-house

Washington State School for the Blind
2214 E. 13th St [1906]
clark.wa.gov/community-planning/
washington-state-school-blind

Peter J. Flynn House
114 W. 20th St [1926]
clark.wa.gov/community-planning/
peter-j-flynn-house

Swan House
714 E. 26th St [1906]
clark.wa.gov/community-planning/
swan-house

Albert M. Munger House
112 W. 28th St [1926]
clark.wa.gov/community-planning/
albert-m-munger-house

Propstra House
220 W. 36th St [1923]
clark.wa.gov/community-planning/
propstra-house

Gaiser House
313 W. 36th St [1935]
clark.wa.gov/community-planning/
paul-gaiser-house

Clark County Poor Farm
1919 NE 78th St [1913]
clark.wa.gov/community-planning/
clark-county-poor-farm

Birrer Barn
8612 NE 119th St [1953]
clark.wa.gov/community-planning/
birrer-barn

Luigi & Louisa Podesta Farm
7804 NE 139th St [1950]
clark.wa.gov/community-planning/
luigi-louisa-podesta-farm

Historic Hough Neighborhood
[1890-1945]
clark.wa.gov/community-planning/
hough-neighborhood-historic-district

Columbian Building
110 E Evergreen Blvd [c. 1928]
clark.wa.gov/community-planning/
columbian-building

Ford Corner Dealership
204 W Evergreen Blvd
[1920 and 1929]
clark.wa.gov/community-planning/
ford-corner-dealership

Salvation Army Building
311 W Evergreen Blvd [1952]
clark.wa.gov/community-planning/
salvation-army-building

House of Providence
400 E Evergreen Blvd [1873]
clark.wa.gov/community-planning/
house-providence

Officers Row Historic District
611 E Evergreen Blvd [1849]
clark.wa.gov/community-planning/
officers-row-historic-district

Cushing-Caples House
712 W Evergreen Blvd [c. 1888]
clark.wa.gov/community-planning/
cushing-caples-house

Grant House
1101 E Evergreen Blvd [c. 1886]
clark.wa.gov/community-planning/
grant-house

Amboy
Amboy United Brethren Church
21416 NE 399th St [1900]
northclarkhistoricalmuseum.org

Enoch Hazen Barn
121000 NE Grantham Rd [1888]
clark.wa.gov/community-planning/
enoch-hazen-barn

Tum Tum Springs Dairy
31908 NE Healy Rd [1900]
clark.wa.gov/community-planning/
tum-tum-springs-dairy

Battle Ground
Rieck House
312 E Main St [c. 1927]
clark.wa.gov/community-planning/
rieck-house

Jacob Schwartz Barn
6505 NE 209th St [1917]
clark.wa.gov/community-planning/
jacob-schwartz-barn

Venersborg School
24309 NE 209th St [c. 1912]
clark.wa.gov/community-planning/
venersborg-school

Henry Heisen House
17316 NE 279th St [c. 1898]
clark.wa.gov/community-planning/
henry-heisen-house

Henry Heisen Farm
27904 NE 174th Ave [1898]
clark.wa.gov/community-planning/
heisen-henry-farm

Ander Moberg Barn
20309 NE 242nd Ave [1918]
clark.wa.gov/community-planning/
ander-moberg-barn

Jacob & Sophie Lahti Farm
21406 NE 167th Ave [1925]
clark.wa.gov/community-planning/
jacob-sophie-lahti-farm

Burdoin House
18609 NE Cramer Rd [c. 1903]
clark.wa.gov/community-planning/
burdoin-house

Dr Albert and Letha Green Barn
12112 NE Gren Fels [c. 1900]
clark.wa.gov/community-planning/
albert-and-letha-green-barn

Albert and Letha Green House
25716 NE Lewisville Hwy [c. 1885]
clark.wa.gov/community-planning/
albert-and-letha-green-house

Lewisville Park
26411 NE Lewisville Hwy [c. 1936]
clark.wa.gov/public-works/lewis-
ville-regional-park

Brush Prairie

Bertha "Bertie" Fifield House
15716 NE 112th Ave [c. 1912]
clark.wa.gov/community-planning/
bertha-bertie-fifield-house

Kapus Granary
15716 NE 112th Ave [c. 1929]
clark.wa.gov/community-planning/
kapus-granary

Henry & Ann Poeland Farm
19432 NE Mattson Rd [1959]
clark.wa.gov/community-planning/
henry-ann-poeland-farm

Kelsey Family Farm
19432 NE Mattson Rd
kelseyfamilyfarm.com

Camas

Leadbetter House
1317 NE Everett St [c. 1909]
clark.wa.gov/community-planning/
pittock-leadbetter-house

John Roffler House
1437 NE Everett St [c. 1906]
clark.wa.gov/community-planning/
john-roffler-house

Johnson House
526 NE Hayes St [c. 1911]
clark.wa.gov/community-planning/
johnson-house

Farrell House
416 NE Ione St [c.1915]
clark.wa.gov/community-planning/
farrell-house

American Legion Hall Post #27
1554 NE 3rd Ave [1935]
clark.wa.gov/community-planning/
american-legion-hall-post-27-0

Charlie and Rose Farrell Building
305 NE 4th Ave [c. 1924]
clark.wa.gov/community-planning/
charlie-and-rose-farrell-building

Camas Main Post Office
440 NE 5th Ave [c. 1939]
clark.wa.gov/community-planning/
camas-main-post-office

La Center

Charles and Frances Zener House
1411 NE Lockwood Creek Rd
[1907]
clark.wa.gov/community-planning/
zener-house-charles-and-frances

Francis G. Lawton House
5404 NE Lockwood Creek Rd
[c. 1900]
clark.wa.gov/community-planning/
francis-g-lawton-house

Ridgefield

Basalt Cobblestone Quarries
NW Main St and NW 291st St
[c. 1880]
clark.wa.gov/community-planning/
basalt-cobblestone-quarries

Ridgefield City Hall
230 Pioneer St [1920]
clark.wa.gov/community-planning/
ridgefield-city-hall-ridgefield-state-
bank-listed-county-heritage-register

Charles J. Nickels Barn
2929 NW 199th St [1939]
clark.wa.gov/community-planning/
charles-j-nickels-barn

Arndt Prune Dryer
2109 NW 219th St
[c. 1898 and expanded]
clark.wa.gov/community-planning/
arndt-prune-dryer

Hilltop Farm
6600 NW 287th St [1900]
clark.wa.gov/community-planning/
hilltop-farm

Dr. Ralph & Florence Stryker House
207 S 3rd Ave [c. 1912]
clark.wa.gov/community-planning/
dr-ralph-and-florence-stryker-house

McCormick Barn
29117 NE 10th Ave [1915]
clark.wa.gov/community-planning/
mccormick-barn

Lambert School
21814 NW 11th Ave [c. 1926]
clark.wa.gov/community-planning/
lambert-school

Bottlemillers Barn
22319 NW 11th Ave [1926]
clark.wa.gov/community-planning/
bottlemillers-barn

Kampe Prune Dryer
16516 W 41st Ave [1907]
clark.wa.gov/community-planning/
kampe-prune-dryer

Sara Store
17903 NW 41st Ave [c. 1880s]
clark.wa.gov/community-planning/
sara-store

Kapus Farm
745 N 65th Ave [c. 1888]
clark.wa.gov/community-planning/
kapus-farm

Shobert House
621 Shobert Ln [c. 1905-1907]
clark.wa.gov/community-planning/
shobert-house

Judge Lancaster Columbia House
33415 NW Lancaster Rd   [c. 1850]
clark.wa.gov/community-planning/
judge-lancaster-columbia-house

Lancaster Farm
33415 NW Lancaster Rd
[c. 1880 c. 1950]
clark.wa.gov/community-planning/
lancaster-farm

Roth Dairy
21310 NW Roth Rd [1917]
clark.wa.gov/community-planning/
roth-dairy

Summit Grove Lodge
30810 NE Timmen Rd [c. 1927]
summitgrovelodge.net

Hidden House

Things to Do Index

Antiques

Trash or treasure? When do secondhand, used, or hand-me-down objects take on a new identity and become someone's most valued find? Hmmm, not sure, but here is a list of places where you can start making your own evaluations or start a project to transform something old into something new.

Fabulous Flippin' Treasures
10am-6pm
Vintage Mall, 2519 E 4th Plain Blvd
flippin-treasures.com
360-200-8045

House of Vintage
Daily 11am-6pm
1501 Main St
houseofvintagenw.com/vancouver
360-694-1991

Main St. Vintage
1803 Main St
mainstvintage.com
360-719-2592

Old Glory Antiques & Vintage
2000 Main St
facebook.com/oldgloryantique-sandvintage
360-906-8823

Persnickety
1911 Main St
facebook.com/persnicketyvintage
530-481-5997

Reliques Marketplace
7601 NE Vancouver Plaza Dr
7809 NE Vancouver Plaza Dr, Ste 230B
facebook.com/reliquesmarketplace
360-254-1402

Urban Barnhouse
1333 Washington St
facebook.com/UrbanBarnhouse
360-695-9870

Arcades

Is coin-operated fun still a thing? Why would you want to drop clinking change or dollars into a machine when you can simply download a new app on your phone? Perhaps it's just because it's fun? Something you can yell, scream, moan, and groan about in an environment where that is all perfectly acceptable, thank you very much. Let the games begin!

Allen's Crosley Lanes
2400 E Evergreen Blvd
crosleylanes.com
360-693-4789

Big Al's
16615 SE 18th St
ilovebigals.com/vancouver
360-944-6118

Chuck E. Cheese
7721 NE Vancouver Plaza Dr
chuckecheese.com
360-896-6672

Husted's Hazel Dell Lanes
6300 NE Hwy 99
hazeldelllanes.com
360-694-8364

Vault 31 Bar
Video Game Lounge
4,600 games in collection, though not all available at same time.
316 SE 123rd Ave, D4
vault31bar.com
360-828-8980

Bands

Music opens an emotion of sound that changes how we feel, think and even act. Whether its the beat of the drum or the strum of the guitar good musicians hold a magical power to transport an ordinary moment into a new dimension. Explore new places and spaces where this magic happens.

Live

99 Saloon & Grill
7005 NE Hwy 99
99saloon.wixsite.
com/99saloonandgrill
360-693-8125

Back Alley Bar & Grill
E Mill Plain Blvd, Ste D
thebackalleyonline.com/home.html
360-694-6873

Billy Blues Bar & Grill
7115 NE Hazel Dell Ave
billybluesbarandgrill.com
360-694-3114

Brick House
109 W 15th St
vancouverbrickhouse.com
360-695-3686

Cascade Bar & Grill
15000 SE Mill Plain Blvd
cascadebarandgrill.net
360-254-0749

Final Draft Taphouse
11504 Mill Plain Blvd
finaldrafttaphouse.com
360-433-9966

Frontier Public House Restaurant
4909 NE Hazel Dell Ave
frontierpublichouse.com
360-718-2768

Growler Rush
16320 SE Cascade Park Dr
growlerrush.com
360-891-1076

The Heavy Metal Pizza & Brewing Co.
809 MacArthur Blvd
theheavymetalbrewingco.com
360-258-1691

Hudson's Bar and Grill
Piano
7805 NE Greenwood Dr
hudsonsbarandgrill.com
360-816-6100

Latte Da Coffee House and Wine Bar
205 E 39th St
lattedacoffeehouse.com
360-448-7651

Locust Cider & Brewing
700 Washington St #103
locustcider.com/taprooms/vancouver
360-984-6963

Loowit Brewing Company
507 Columbia St
loowitbrewing.com
360-566-2323

Lucky's Roadhouse
9306 NE 76th St
360-984-6430

McMenamins on the Columbia
1801 SE Columbia River Dr
mcmenamins.com/mcmenamins-on-the-columbia/home
360-699-1521

One Eighty Concert Cafe
2525 E 4th Plain Blvd

Shanahan's Pub & Grill
209 W McLoughlin Blvd
shanahanspubvancouver.com
360-735-1440

Sport Bar & Grill
Local music Fri-Sat 7pm-9pm
7225 NE Fourth Plain Blvd
facebook.com/thespotvancouver
360-256-1110

Tap Union Freehouse
1300 Washington St #200
tapunionfreehouse.com
360-726-6921

Three Monkeys Bar and Grill
7917 NE Hwy 99
3monkeysbarandgrill.com
360-314-6201

Baseball

"Many historians credit the US Army for the spread of baseball throughout the country. On May 11, 1867, an organized team of soldiers from the Army's Fort Vancouver –dubbed the "Garrison Boys" by the press –played the Occidental Base Ball Club of Vancouver, with the soldiers winning by a score of 45 to 5."
nps.gov/fova/learn/news/baseball2015.htm

Adult Teams

Southwest Washington Adult Baseball League
Currently 7 teams in the 45+ division and 6 teams in the 35+ division. Games are played on Sundays in SW Washington.
Mailing Address: 15640 NE Fourth Plain Blvd Ste #106, PMB 56 Vancouver, WA 98682
swabl.com

Northwest Independent Baseball League
18+ Semi-Pro & Adult Baseball for NW Oregon and SW Washington.
nwibl.org

Fields

Chieftain Field
Columbia River High School
800 NW 99th Street
river.vansd.org
360-313-3900

Salmon Creek Little League Field
Luke Jensen Sports Park, 4000 NE 78th St
salmoncreekll.com
360-887-8964

Little League

Cascade Little League
NE 18th St & NE 192nd Ave
cascadelittleleague.org
360-818-4471

Columbia Little League
900 N Garrison Rd
columbiall.org
360-696-1278

Fort Vancouver Little League
1301 E Mill Plain Blvd
fortvancouverlittleleague.org
360-696-2994

Salmon Creek Little League Field
Luke Jensen Sports Park, 4000 NE 78th St
salmoncreekll.com
360-887-8964

Beading

Beads made of wood, stone, shells and bone were a valued trade item for Native Americans in the Pacific Northwest and throughout the country for hundreds probably thousands of years. Europeans introduced glass beads as trade items which expanded their beadwork allowing them to more intricate and beautiful designs for clothing, belts and jewlery.

Hobby Lobby
8800 NE Vancouver Mall Dr #120
hobbylobby.com
360-254-1776

Michaels
16601 SE Mill Plain Blvd
michaels.com
360-892-4494

Joann
11505 NE Fourth Plain Blvd Ste B
joann.com
360-254-1100

7907 NE Highway 99
joann.com
360-573-1407

Add Notes

Biking

The first bikes showed up in Vancouver in the 1800s and quickly became a popular mode of transportation. In Vancouver, you can find bike maps, information, and fellow enthusiasts.

Bike Clark County
1604 Main Street
bikeclarkcounty.org

AllTrails.com
The best road biking trails in Vancouver and beyond.
alltrails.com/us/washington/vancouver/road-biking

Bicycle Maps
The City of Vancouver provides 15+ bike maps of the area.
cityofvancouver.us/ced/page/bicycle-maps

Road and Biking Adventures
Brief introduction to the most popular biking around Vancouver.
visitvancouverusa.com/things-to-do/outdoor-recreation/biking

Biking Near Vancouver

Map My Ride
Vancouver cycling trails.
mapmyride.com/us/vancouver-wa

Mountain bike trails
mtbproject.com/directory/8011608/vancouver

Vancouver Bicycle Club
RACC Ride around Clark County
vbc-usa.com
360-519-7605

Mountain Bike Trails

MTB Project – Vancouver
An extensive crowd-sourced project of bike trails by locals.
mtbproject.com/directory/8011608/vancouver

Online and downloadable map for Cycling the City of Vancouver.

Billiards (Pool)

This game has been around for five or six centuries. In Vancouver, the earliest record I've found was in 1886, when a table was provided for soldiers' recreation at the Canteen to keep them happy at the barracks and cause less trouble off base. In 1919, the American Red Cross provided a billiards table for recovering soldiers at Vancouver Barracks. Today, you can find local pool tournament information at sharkshooter.net

4th Plain Tavern
13206 NE Fourth Plain Blvd
4thplaintavern.com
360-254-3729

99 Saloon
7005 NE Hwy 99
99saloon.wixsite.
com/99saloonandgrill
360-693-8125

Auto's Pub
16209 SE Mcgillivray Blvd
autos-pub.com
360-253-6253

Back Alley Bar & Grill
6503 E Mill Plain Blvd Ste E
thebackalleyonline.com
360-694-6873

Big Al's
16615 SE 18th St
ilovebigals.com/vancouver
360-944-6118

Charlie's Sports Bar & Grill
3315 NE 112th Ave
charliessportsbar.com

Cascade Bar & Grill
15000 SE Mill Plain Blvd
cascadebarandgrill.net
360-254-0749

Double Barrel Tap House
8308 NE Highway 99
doublebarreltaphouse.com
360-433-9867

Jakes Bar & Grill
4602 NE Saint Johns Road
jakesbarandgrill.com
360-696-3727

Korner Street Bar & Grill
6403 NE St Johns Rd
360-735-9009

Lucky's Roadhouse
9306 NE 76th St
360-984-6430

The Off Ramp Sports Bar & Grill
400 NE 112th Ave 5018
theofframpsportsbar.com
360-326-3472

Sellberg's Tavern
2110 St Johns Blvd
sellbergs-tavern.edan.io
360-695-1854

Shanahan's Pub & Grill
209 W McLoughlin Blvd
shanahanspubvancouver.com
360-735-1440

Silver Star Saloon
6718 NE Fourth Plain Blvd
silver-star-saloon.business.site
360-694-5742

Spot Bar & Grill
7225 NE Fourth Plain Blvd
spotbargrill.com
360-256-1110

Bird-watching

Birding or bird-watching is an activity that can be enjoyed by all ages. Bird-watchers have photographed more than 200 different birds in Clark County, not including those at Ridgefield National Wildlife Refuge.

Backyard Bird Shop Vancouver
Everything to attract birds and wildlife to your backyard.
8101 NE Parkway
backyardbirdshop.com
360-253-5771

Bird Calls
Audio recordings of Clark County birds can be found by going to
clark.wa.gov

Birding Pal
A place to connect with other birding contacts and bird-watching information.
birdingpal.org/wa.htm

Birding Washington State
A state checklist of approximately 500 birds species found in Washington.
birdingwashington.info

Common backyard birds
in Washington. A list of 30 common birds found in local neighborhoods.
whatbirdsareinmybackyard.com/2019/09/what-are-most-common-backyard-birds-in-washington.html

Northwest Birding – Clark County
A listing of birds seen, heard, or photographed iwn Clark County.
northwestbirding.com/ClarkCo/index.html

Ridgefield National Wildlife Refuge
The refuge is a beautiful nature retreat to see birds; it is nestled between the Columbia River and the town of Ridgefield.

Carty Unit: 28908 NW Main Ave Ridgefield
River S Unit: 1071 S Hilhurst Rd, Ridgefield
fws.gov/refuge/Ridgefield/visit/plan_your_visit.html

Vancouver Audubon Society
A birding resource for the entire state of Washington.
vancouveraudubon.org/local-birding

Boating

If you live near the water, then it only makes sense you should spend at least some "time" on the water. And when you live along the Columbia River, the largest North American river (approximately 1,243 miles long) flowing into the Pacific Ocean . . . well . . . it's definitely water time! See also Kayaking and Canoes *(pg 133)*.

Clubs

Island Sailing Club & School
Provides training and coaching of seamanship by coast guard licensed captains.
islandsailing.org

Vancouver Lake Sailing Club
Promotes sailing and racing of one-design centerboard boats.
vlsc.org

Vancouver Lake Rowing Club
For youth and adult rowers including at risk individuals by teaching rowing, water safety and team building.
vancouverlakerowingclub.com
206-450-3433

Marinas/Boat Ramps
Felida Moorage
Provides moorage for fishing and houseboats on the Lake River near Vancouver Lake.
felidamoorage.com
360-573-3394

McCuddy's Steamboat Landing Marina
Provides 150 floating concrete slips for 24' to 40' boats within a gated community.
mccuddysmarina.com/steamboat-landing
360-254-1000

Tidewater Cove Marina
Provides slips for 45' to 85' boats in Vancouver, north of the Columbia River.
tidewatercovemarina.com
360-977-2015

Vancouver Lake Boat Ramp
Water access areas provided by the Washington Department of Fish and Wildlife (WDFW).
wdfw.wa.gov/places-to-go/water-access-sites

Rentals

Portland Electric Boat Company
1811 S River Dr Suite 400, Portland, OR 97201
portlandelectricboatco.com
503-673-6172

Yacht Charter PDX
2001 SW River Dr Portland, OR
yachtcharterpdx.com
503-877-4842

Boatyards

Christensen Yachts
4400 SE Columbia Way
christensenyachts.com
360-831-9800

Book Clubs

One of the first books groups in Vancouver was started at the Vancouver Barracks. Grant House, built in 1849 while housing the commander of the fort, was also the center for a small library for use by Army officers.

The Fort Vancouver Library

(FVRL)offers book clubs at its different branches.

fvrl.org
360-906-5000

FVRL Book Clubs

Catch Up With the Classics
1st Wed Morning Book Group
Kids Book Group
Nature Lovers Book Group
2nd Tue Morning Book Group
Y.A. (Young Adult) for the Olds

Luepke Community Center

1009 E McLoughlin Blvd
cityofvancouver.us/marshall
360-487-7100

Add Notes

Red Herring Mystery Book Club

2nd Mon 1pm-3pm
360-487-7084

Vancouver Book Club

(All Genres)
meetup.com/vancouverbookclub

Bowling

The American version of ten pin bowling is an adaption of the German nine pin game, which, in the 1830s, was considered a rather low, immoral game found in saloons. A few cities made laws against it, but by adding one more "pin" to the game, it no longer fell under those established laws, and bowling aficionados returned to their play.

Allen's Crosley Lanes

2400 E Evergreen Blvd
crosleylanes.com
360-693-4789

Big Al's

16615 SE 18th St
ilovebigals.com/vancouver
360-944-6118

Baileys Tiger Bowl

211 N Parkway Ave, Battle Ground
baileystigerbowl.com
360-723-0082

Husted's Hazel Dell Lanes

6300 NE Hwy 99
hazeldelllanes.com
360-694-8364

League Secretary

An online resource that provides bowlers with statistical information behind their bowling.

leaguesecretary.com

Cars

The first cars to appear in Vancouver were driven over the bridge by adventurous Portlanders. A number of Vancouvers were highly indignant that such contraptions were allowed to horrify decent folks as well as scare horses into mad runaways. One crazy Portland woman was ticketed and fined severely for such misbehavior.

In time, though, even Vancouver got with the times to the point that the Vancouver Barracks actually allowed car club members to drive through the barracks as long as they did not go over 10 miles an hour.

Car Clubs

BCA Prewar Division

BCA (Buick Club of America) Promotes restoration, touring, and special events for prewar Buicks.

classiccarcommunity.com/car-club/bca+pre-war+division/3037

360-573-2823

Evergreen Mustangs

Car club for Ford Mustangs.

Camas

evergreenmustangs.weebly.com

Hotrod Hotline Northwest

Extensive information for cars of all makes and models that are for sale, parts, and car shows.

hotrodhotline.com/content/club-listings-northwest

NW Corvette

Car club for Corvettes

nwcorvette.com

Old Rides

A listing of Washington State car clubs.

oldride.com/clubs/washington-clubs.html

Pharaohs Street Rodders (Portland/Vancouver)

Car club for hot rod, classic, antique, and special interest vehicles in the Portland / Vancouver area.

pharaohsstreetrodders.com/about.html

503-789-1965

Car Shows

Classic Car Show

Camas

June

downtowncamas.com/event/camas-car-show

Harvest Nights Car Cruise
July
Battle Ground
battlegroundfestivals.com

Our Days
La Center
See event calendar for July
facebook.com/LaCenterOurDays-
Celebration

PDX Car Culture
Start here to find the latest car
shows in the Portland/Vancouver
metro.
pdxcarculture.com/events

Concerts

Vancouver's music scene was
vibrant as far back as the mid-
1850s, when the Covington House
came alive with piano, violin, and
frequent sing-along guests—including Ulysses S. Grant. Today,
concerts continue to be popular
with full orchestration, professional
conductors, and artists presenting a
wide variety of musical themes and
performances.

Indoor

Bravo! Concerts
Bravo! is a 501c3 nonprofit arts
corporation based in southwest
Washington. It presents sacred,
classical, jazz, pop, contemporary,
American, and chamber music
concert series.
bravoconcerts.com/home.html
360-906-0441

ilani Resort
Events include concerts, dance performances, comedy shows, sport-
ing events, and live shows.
1 Cowlitz Way, Ridgefield
ilaniresort.com/poi/venues/cowlitz-
ballroom.html
877-464-5264

Metropolitan Performing Arts
A local performing arts school.
metropolitanperformingarts.org
360-975-1585

Public Concerts at Clark
Beacock Music Hall
Clark college presents choral, jazz,
and music concerts.
clark.edu/campus-life/arts-events/
music/index.php
360-992-2662

T-Wolf Choir
The Heritage Senior High School
choir concerts.
twolfchoir.com/tw
360-604-3400

Vancouver Symphony Orchestra
The orchestra celebrates 43-plus
years of providing symphonic music to the community. Venues are
held at different locations throughout the year.
vancouversymphony.org
360-735-7278

Outdoor

The first band to perform in Vancouver was the regimental band that accompanied the Fourth Regiment in 1852. In 1865, it was reported that the regimental band played every evening for Vancouver's officers, families, and residents at the Parade Ground Bandstand, as well as performed for special occasions, balls, and musical gatherings. Vancouver continues the tradition with free summer concerts at Esther Short Park (Fridays) and the Columbia Tech Center (Sundays), as well as fun, family-friendly music performed at the Farmer's Markets on weekends.

County Fair Concert

Concert events with grandstand seating during August County Fair.
Clark County Fairgrounds
17402 NE Delfel Rd, Ridgefield
clarkcofair.com/fair-concerts.html
564-397-6180

RV Inn Style Resorts Amphitheater

Live Nation events with the country's leading performers and top venues.
17200 NE Delfel Rd, Ridgefield
livenation.com/venue/KovZpZA-Jld6A/rv-inn-style-resorts-amphitheater-events
360-816-7000

Vancouver Wine and Jazz Festival

"Features internationally acclaimed jazz, blues, gospel, and pop musicians, Northwest wines, fine art, food, exhibits, and fun."
Typically the last Fri-Sun in August
vancouverwinejazz.com
360-906-0441

Free in Vancouver

Sunday Sounds Concert Series

Presented by Columbia Tech Center and iQ Credit Union.
Every Sun 6pm-8pm Jul-Aug
Amphitheater at Columbia Tech Center Park, SE Sequoia Circle at SE Tech Center Drive
cityofvancouver.us/parksrecculture/page/summer-concert-series

Waterfront Park Concert Series

Presented by Riverview Community Bank
Every Fri 6pm-8pm Jul-Aug
695 Waterfront Way
cityofvancouver.us/parksrecculture/page/summer-concert-series

Free in Portland

A short drive across the river opens up a medley of summer concerts at parks around Portland, OR, almost every day of the week.
portland.gov/parks/arts-culture/sffa

Casinos

ilani
1 Cowlitz Wy Ridgefield
ilaniresort.com
877-464-5264

The Last Frontier Casino
105 W 4th St La Center
thelastfrontiercasino.com
360-573-6442

New Phoenix Casino
225 W 4th St La Center
thenewphoenixcasino.com
503-281-0932

Palace Casino
318 NW Pacific Hwy La Center
nwcasinos.com
360-263-2988

Cooking Classes

Class Cooking
Chef Kim's small-group gourmet
cooking classes offer students
an enjoyable, hands-on learning
experience.
class-cooking.com/classes
360-600-8006

Northwest Culinary Institute
2901 E Mill Plain Blvd
northwestculinary.com
877-341-5525

PDX Munch Time
7803 NE Fourth Plain Blvd (in Sea
Mar Family Housing)
pdxmunchtime.com
360-524-2413

**The Tod and Maxine McClas-
key Culinary Institute**
Cuisine at Clark College
Lessons in production kitchen,
retail bakery, food kiosks, and a
full-service dining room.
Degrees & Certificates
1933 Fort Vancouver Way
clark.edu/academics/programs/
business-and-entrepreneurship/cui-
sine/index.php
360-699-6398

Craft Brews

The first craft brews in the
Pacific Northwest had a British
touch. Once again we refer to Dr.
John McLoughlin and the HBC.
As early as 1826 field crops were
started to supply food and shortly
after a small portion (wheat and
barley)set aside for beer making.
Within a few years brew production increased to the point it could
be exported and sent to other forts
in the HBC system.

Ben's Bottle Shop
Restaurant and Tap Room
8052 E Mill Plain Blvd 2002
bensbottleshop.com
360-314-6209

Brewed Cafe & Pub
603 Main St
brewedcafepub.com
360-597-3386

Brother Ass Brewing
11700 NE 54th Cr
brotherassbrewing.com
360-607-3275

Brothers Cascadia Brewing
9811 NE 15th Ave
brotherscascadiabrewing.com
360-718-8927

Doomsday Brewing
Ben's Bottle Shop
Restaurant and Tap Room
8052 E Mill Plain Blvd 2002
bensbottleshop.com
360-314-6209

Brewed Cafe & Pub
603 Main St
brewedcafepub.com
360-597-3386

Brother Ass Brewing
11700 NE 54th Ct
brotherassbrewing.com
360-607-3275

Brothers Cascadia Brewing
9811 NE 15th Ave
brotherscascadiabrewing.com
360-718-8927

Doomsday Brewing
1919 Main St
doomsdaybrewing.com
360-335-9909

Double Barrel Taphouse
8308 NE Hwy 99
doublebarreltaphouse.com _
360-433-9867

Final Draft Taphouse
11504 Mill Plain Blvd
finaldrafttaphouse.com
360-433-9966

Fortside Brewing Company
2200 NE Andresen Rd
fortsidebrewing.com
360-524-4692

Ghost Runners Brewery &
Kitchen
4216 NE Minnehaha St #108
ghostrunnersbrewery.com
360-989-3912

Heathen Brewing Feral Public
House
1109 Washington St
heathenbrewing.com
360-836-5255

Heavy Metal Pizza Brewing Co
809 MacArthur Blvd
theheavymetalbrewingco.com
360 258-1691

Hopworks Urban Brewery
17707 SE Mill Plain Blvd
hopworksbeer.com
360-828-5139

Loowit Brewing Company
507 Columbia S
loowitbrewing.com
360-566-2323

Brothers Cascadia Evergreen
Pub
108 W Evergreen Blvd
mavsbrewing.com
360-726-6914

Railside Brewery
309 NE 76th St
360-907-8582

Trap Door Brewing
2315 Main St
trapdoorbrewing.com
360-314-6966

Trusty Brewing Company
114 E Evergreen Blvd
trustybrewing.com
360-258-0413

Victor 23 Brewing
2905 St Johns Blvd
victor23.com
360-984-5413

Waterfront Taphouse
801 Waterfront Way, Ste 203
thewaterfronttaphouse.com
360-719-2043

Craft Brew Fests

Craft Beer & Wine Fest
This 21+ (ID checked) event is three days of live music, brews, handmade beer, and wine-themed crafts; it has become one of Vancouver's most loved celebrations.
Jul (last week)
$27-$39
811 Main St
thecraftwinefest.com
425-698-3236

Oregon and SW Washington Beer Festival Guide
newschoolbeer.com/home/2021/6/oregon-beer-festival-calendar-guide

Crafting

Making articles by hand is a developed skill creating elements as artwork or for use in the home, business or outdoors. *See also needlework*

A few basic resources for classes, workshops and supplies.

Craft Warehouse
Columbia Square
13503-A SE Mill Plain Blvd
craftwarehouse.com
360-892-2277

Hazel Dell Towne Center
9307 NE 5th Ave
craftwarehouse.com
360-828-1030

Hobby Lobby
8800 NE Vancouver Mall Dr #120
hobbylobby.com
360-254-1776

JOANN Fabric and Crafts
7907 NE Hwy 99
joann.com
360-573-1407

11505 NE Fourth Plain Blvd Ste 86
joann.com
360-254-1100

Kilnfolk
Clay studio and Gallery. Pottery classes and painting. Day & Evening hours.
108 W 6th St
kilnfolkclay.com
360-900-1731

Live Laugh Love Art
Open studio for glass fusing, canvas and pottery painting and more. Classes and workshops.
17707 SE Mill Plain Blvd
livelaughloveart.com/vancouver
360-787-7033

Melt Glass
Glass making classes and supplies
502 Washington St
meltglass.com
360-771-5617

Michaels
16601 SE Mill Plain Blvd
michaels.com
360-892-4494

Add Notes

Dance

All cultures embrace dancing as a celebration to connect the joy of being alive in body and spirit.

Adult Instruction

Arthur Murray Dance Center
808 SE Chkalov Dr, Ste 9
arthurmurrayvancouver.com
360-699-4500

Carole Duttinger
Specializes in West Coast swing, East Coast swing, nightclub two-step and country two-step, as well as line dancing.
cduttlinger.wixsite.com/dance
509-670-0435

CJ's Country Dance Instruction
Silver Star Saloon, 6718 E 4th Plain
cjscountrydance.com

Dance Evolution
Dance academy and adult fitness with Zumba Gold and UJam Fitness.
1004 NE 4th Ave, Camas
danceevolutionfitness.com/zumba
360-818-1695

Dance Lessons - Daniel Martinez
Private or group ballroom lessons in the six major dances: waltz, tango, foxtrot, rumba, cha cha, swing, and Latin-dance styles, including salsa, Bachata, merengue, samba or hip-hop, jazz, and contemporary.
1515 Grant St
dancewithdanny.com
360-607-3627

Happy Hoppers
Square dance lessons with Jim Hattrick. Washington Grange
82–7701 NE Ward Rd
happy-hoppers.com
360-573-0522

Luepke Center
Offers aerobic/dance studio for senior fitness and wellness.
1009 E McLoughlin Blvd
cityofvancouver.us/messenger/page/luepke-center
360-487-7090

Studio Pole 4 Fun
Offers a rotating schedule of group classes, private lessons, workshops, and parties to learn and have fun pole dancing.
9014 NE St. Johns Rd, Ste 112
pole4fun.com

Xpression Studio Zumba
facebook.com/xpresionconmarisol

A New Dance Experience

Workshop and competition dancing for ages 5-13+.

4120 NE 45th Ave
newdanceexperience.com
503-653-7748

Claudette Walker Dance

A large variety of dance classes offered through the year, with individual or group sessions progressing to public performances for small and large. They also offer a two-week summer camp.

7406 Delaware Ln
claudettewalkerdance.net
360-694-1192

Columbia Dance

High-quality ballet and other dance classes for children and adults in a non-competitive, fun environment.

columbiadance.org
360-737-1922

Dance Evolution

Youth and adult.

1004 NE 4th Ave, Camas
danceevolutionfitness.com
360-818-1695

Dance Works

Technical classes in ballet, jazz, and contemporary.

Ages 3 to adult.

11005 NE Fourth Plain Blvd
danceworksperformingarts.com
360-892-5664

Evergreen Dance Academy

Ballet, jazz, hip-hop, and tap. Ages 3 to adult.

2100 SE 164th Ave, Ste D-111
evergreendanceacademy.com
360-450-0244

Kids Club Fun & Fitness

Dance, Gymnastics, Swimming Ages 2 1/2 to 12

13914 NW 3rd Ct
kidsclub4fun.com/lessons/dance/

Groove Nation Performing Arts Center

Dance and music lessons (youth to young adult) and birthday parties.

3000 Columbia House Blvd 107
groovenationdance.com
360-699-7150

Jennifer Santos School

Academy of Dance

Offers dance classes, including ballet, tap, jazz, and beginning tumbling

3414 NE 52nd St, Ste B106
jennifersantosacademyofdance.com
360-901-6006

Liz Borromeo Dance Studio

Ballet, tap, and jazz for students, along with educational and problem-solving skills.

404 E Evergreen Blvd
lizborromeodance.com
360-281-3280

Meiya Dance School
Master of Chinese dance, ballet, and folk dance, as well as yoga, jazz, and zumba.
3200 SE 164th Ave 222
meiyadance.com
360-931-5667

Northwest Classical Ballet
Classical education in ballet for both new dancers and seasoned performers.
14511 NE 10th Ave, Ste D
northwestclassicalballet.com
360-883-9656

Ora Nui Tahitian Dance Studio
Learn authentic Tahitian dance, with fast-moving hips and rhythmic drum beats.
9312 NE 76th St
oranui.com
808-421-7760

Pulse Dance Studio
Learn ballet, jazz, lyrical, contemporary, tap, hip-hop, technique, acro, stretch, and pointe, with competition and options. Ages 3+.
3200 SE 164th Ave
pulsedancenw.com
360-953-3725

Riverside Performing Arts
An all-inclusive dance, theater, and music-training academy and preschool. Teaches ages 2 to adult, from beginner to pre-professional.
1307 NE 78th St
riversidepa.com
360-694-8662

VanCity Ballroom
A venue for ballroom, Latin, and swing dancing, with a beginning 45-minute lesson before the dancing begins.
9212 NE Hwy 99, Ste 108/110
vancityballroom.com/events
360-907-4694

Dance–Social

See also Band-Live

Billy Blues Bar and Grill
A fun and happy place to hang out with live music (check calendar) and dance floor. Cover charges on some Fridays and Saturdays.
billybluesbarandgrill.com
360-694-3114

Portland Dance
Simple list of dancing venues in the Portland-Vancouver metro.
Ballroom, country, Irish, salsa, tango, waltz, and others.
portlanddancing.com

VanCity Ballroom
Beginner lessons and social dancing.
9212 NE Hwy 99
vancityballroom.com
360-907-4694
Add Notes

Farm Fresh

Looking for fresh eggs, vegetables, and fruits? A good place to start is at a website called Local Harvest. It lists farms, farm stands, and farmer's markets across the country. There is a good selection for the Vancouver area. Another site for farm produce and free range meat is Get Free Range, listed below.

Bi-Zi Farms

The Zimmerman family farm since 1872 is arguably one of the best known and loved farm markets in the community, with events and great service.

9504 NE 119th St
10am-6pm Apr–Dec
bi-zifarms.com
360-574-9119

Dilish Farm

Offers veggie share every other week from May to November, with in-person pickup.

22904 NE 58th St
dilishfarm.com
360-952-8025 (Patricia Haggerty)

Forward Greens

Indoor vertical farm that grows greens in an earth-friendly and contaminant-free environment. Available in selected local stores (Safeway, Chuck's, etc.) and online.
forwardgreens.com
360-949-7271

Local Harvest
localharvest.org/vancouver-wa

Get Free Range
getfreerange.info/near/ Vancouver,WA/free-range-eggs

Farmers Markets

Vancouver is a little late on the "official" farmer's market scene (1999), though local farmers sold goods first to the Hudson's Bay Company and then the U.S. Army since the mid-1800s. Today, the Downtown Farmer's Market in Vancouver is home to over 250 vendors on a rotating basis and is southwest Washington's No. 1 visitor attraction.

Vancouver Downtown Farmers Market

Sat 9am-3pm, Sun 10am-3pm Mar-Oct
8th and Esther Sts
vancouverfarmersmarket.com

East Vancouver

Thu 10am-2pm Jun-Aug
17701 SE Mill Plain Blvd

Fall Farmer's Market

Sat 9am-2pm Nov-Dec
8th and Esther Sts

Vendors by location: check closer to time.

List of Vendors and Market Days for Downtown Vancouver Farmers Market.

maps.managemymarket.com/5015

CAMAS

Camas Farmer's Market
Wed Jun–Sep
4th Ave between Everett and Franklin
camasfarmersmarket.org
360-838-1032

Other Markets

Night Market
See website for locations
nightmarketvancouver.com

NMV Pop-Local!
111 Grant St
poplocalvancouver.com
360-600-5545
Add Notes

Fishing

See the best fishing spots near Vancouver and in Clark County.
bestfishinginamerica.com/washington-county-clark-fishing-near-vancouver.html

Fishing Regulations for Washington State
wdfw.wa.gov/fishing/regulations

Natural Investment Permit/Discover Pass
parks.wa.gov/470/Natural-Investment-Permit

Two Pole Fishing

Salmon Creek-Klineline Pond
This pond was created from a former gravel pit in the early '70s and stocked with trout for family fishing from the banks. Two-pole fishing is fine with a license, but no floating devices allowed. State residents with fishing license only; youth under 14 free.

Nov-Dec

Parking fees for motorcyles $2, cars and trucks $3 at parking lot
1112 NE 117th St
clark.wa.gov/public-works/salmon-

creek-regional-park/klineline-pond

Types of fish:
Pond bluegill | Brown bullhead | Brown trout | Coastal cutthroat trout (resident) | Common carp | Largemouth bass | Northern pikeminnow | Pumpkinseed sunfish | Rainbow trout

Lacamas Lake

A 312-acre park that has bass, bluegill, and perch. Another small lake, called Round Lake which is located at the southeast end of Lacamas lake provides good bank access for trout and warmwater fishing.
3344 NE Everett St, Camas
wdfw.wa.gov/fishing/locations/lowland-lakes/lacamas-lake

Types of fish:
Black crappie | Bluegill | Brown bullhead | Brown trout | Channel catfish | Common carp | Largemouth | Northern pikeminnow | Pumpkinseed sunfish | Rainbow trout | Warmouth | White sturgeon | Yellow perch

Vancouver Lake

Vancouver Lake, located just west of Vancouver, Washington, is a shallow lake with a maximum depth of 12 to 15 feet deep. Boats are allowed on the lake but must operate with a no-wake speed and not within 200 feet of designated swimming areas. Fees for pulic parking, fishing licenses, and

regulations apply.
clark.wa.gov/public-works/vancouver-lake-regional-park

Types of fish:
American shad | Black crappie | Bluegill | Brown bullhead | Channel catfish | Chiselmouth | Coho salmon | Common carp | Largemouth bass | Northern pikeminnow | Peamouth | Pumpkinseed sunfish | Rainbow trout | Warmouth | White crappie | White sturgeon | Yellow perch

Battle Ground Lake State Park

This 280-acre state park is located 24 miles from Vancouver and 3 miles east of Battle Ground.

The park has an automated pay station to purchase a one-day or annual Discover Pass and boat launch permit. The daily fee to launch a non-motorized watercraft is $7. You will need an annual launch permit (**Natural Investment Permit; or an annual Discover Pass and a daily launch permit; or a one-day Discover Pass and a daily launch permit**).
18002 NE 249th St, Battle Ground
parks.wa.gov/472/Battle-Ground-Lake
360-687-4621

Types of fish:
Lake black crappie | Bluegill | Brown bullhead | Coastal cutthroat trout (resident) | Largemouth bass | Pumpkinseed | Rainbow trout | Warmouth | White sturgeon

Best Fishing in America –Vancouver

An article that highlights "13 Best Fishing Spots Near Vancouver and Clark County".

bestfishinginamerica.com/wash-
ington-county-clark-fishing-near-
vancouver.html

Clark County

bit.ly/3uc1VY0 (WA goverment link)

Fishing and Shellfish Basics

wdfw.wa.gov/fishing/basics

Fishing for crayfish (crawfish)

wdfw.wa.gov/fishing/basics/crayfish

How to dig razor clams

wdfw.wa.gov/fishing/basics/dig-
ging-razor-clams

Identifying crab species and soft-shell crab

wdfw.wa.gov/fishing/basics/crab

Instructional videos

bit.ly/3KVBkEq (YouTube link)

Recreational Salmon Fishing

wdfw.wa.gov/fishing/basics/salmon

Squid fishing

wdfw.wa.gov/fishing/basics/squid

Washington Department of Fish and Wildlife

wdfw.wa.gov

Fitness Centers

Fitness and good health practices are high on the list of many folks in Vancouver. A recent study showed that the closer the fitness center is to your residence, the higher the probability you will continue attending. With this in mind, I have made a rough approximation of listing the centers by location rather than alphabetically, starting with the downtown/uptown area and moving outward.

Note: *Fitness for Seniors is at the end of this listing.*

Downtown/Uptown

Grand Central

2410 Columbia House Blvd, Ste 102
purebarre.com/location/
360-735-7873

CrossFit Fort Vancouver

223 E Reserve St 101
crossfitfortvancouver.com
360-989-7765

Anytime Fitness

710 Esther St
anytimefitness.com
360-635-5350

24 Hour Fitness

800 SE Tech Center Dr
24hourfitness.com/gyms/vancou-
ver-wa/columbia-tech-center-sport
360-514-8381

4th Plain Blvd

LA Fitness
11505 NE 4th Plain Blvd
lafitness.com
360-546-3400

24 Hour Fitness
13019 NE 4th Plain Blvd
24hourfitness.com/gyms/vancouver-wa/vancouver-131st-ave-supersport
360-253-4033

Horizon Sports & Fitness
14602 NE 4th Plain, Ste 1
facebook.com/HorizonSports
360-831-3384

Mill Plain Blvd

Planet Fitness
8024 E Mill Plain Blvd
planetfitness.com/gyms/vancouver-wa
360-448-2277

Location by Street

Precision Personal Training
1012 Washington St 120
precisionptnw.com
360-852-3382

Maxon Fitness
211 E 11th St 203
jenmaxfitness.com
360-566-3600

Cascade Athletic Club
16096 SE 15th St
cascadeac.com/vancouver_
360-597-1100

Lake Shore Athletic Club
2401 NW 94th St
lakeshoreac.com
360-574-1991

Starr Cycle Vancouver
3215 SE 192nd Ave 100
starcycleride.com/studios/vancouver-wa
360 859 3122

Location by Avenue

LA Fitness
7607 NE 5th Ave
lafitness.com
360-546-3400

Jazzercise Vancouver–Vancouver Fitness
7500 NE 16th Ave, 1E
vancouverfitness.us
360-903-1071

Snap Fitness Salmon Creek
14313 NE 20th Ave, 102A
snapfitness.com/us/gyms/salmon-creek-wa
360-433-9338

9 Round 30 Minute Fitness
Kickboxing
2714 NE 114th Ave
9round.com/fitness/vancouver-washington
360-448-7473

Planet Fitness
9919 NE Hazel Dell Ave
planetfitness.com/gyms/hazel-dell-vancouver-wa

LA Fitness
7607 NE 5th Ave
lafitness.com
360-546-3400

Jazzercise Vancouver–Vancouver
Fitness
7500 NE 16th Ave, 1E
vancouverfitness.us
360-903-1071

Snap Fitness Salmon Creek
14313 NE 20th Ave, 102A
snapfitness.com/us/gyms/salmon-
creek-wa
360-433-9338

9 Round 30 Minute Fitness
Kickboxing
2714 NE 114th Ave
9round.com/fitness/vancouver-wash-
ington
360-448-7473

Planet Fitness
9919 NE Hazel Dell Ave
planetfitness.com/gyms/hazel-dell-
vancouver-wa
360-573-4000

The Muscle Bar
4200 NW Fruit Valley Rd, Unit C
thecamptc.com
564-202-4812

Crunch Fitness
7809 NE Vancouver Plaza Dr, Ste 120
crunch.com/locations/vancouver-
plaza

360-256-4193
Gold's Gym Vancouver
8700 NE Vancouver Mall Dr, Ste 220
goldsgym.com/vancouver
360-984-6796

Clark County Family YMCA
11324 NE 51st Cir
ymcacw.org/locations/clark-county-
family-ymca_
360-585-9622

Curves
2702 NE 114th Ave, Ste J-1
curves.com
360-254-5777

Odin's Strength Gym
809 NE Minnehaha St, Hazel Dell
facebook.com/Odinsstrengthgym
508-986-8675

Orange Theory Fitness
7902 NE 6th Ave, Ste 104, Hazel Dell
orangetheory.com
360-851-1108

Snap Fitness Battleground
2312 W Main St, Battle Ground
snapfitness.com/us/gyms/battle-
ground-wa
360-723-0100

Thompson Fitness Center
Clark College Campus 1933 Fort Vancouver Way
clark.edu/campus-life/student-life/
fitness_center
360-992-2808

Fitness for Seniors

Boomer Fitness
516 SE Chkalov Dr
boomerfitness.com
360-597-8079

Fifty and Better
A listing of city of Vancouver programs for seniors.
cityofvancouver.us/parksrecculture/page/fifty-and-better

Firstenburg
700 NE 136th Ave
cityofvancouver.us/firstenburg
360-487-7001

Lake Shore Athletic Club
2401 NW 94th St, Hazel Dell
lakeshoreac.com
360-574-1991

Luepke Center
1009 E McLoughlin Blvd
cityofvancouver.us/messenger/page/luepke-center
360-487-7100

Marshall Community Center
1009 E. McLoughlin Blvd
cityofvancouver.us/marshall_
360-487-7100

Maxon Fitness
Personal fitness.
211 E 11th St 203
jenmaxfitness.com
360-566-3600

Touchmark
2927 SE Village Loop
touchmark.com/senior-living/wa/vancouver/fairway-village/health-fitness-club
360-859-9461

Garage & Estate Sales

Aces Estate Sales
Estate liquidator.
facebook.com/AcesEstateSales
360-609-4875

Clark County Garage Sales
facebook.com/Clark-County-Garage-Sales-202175246471874
360-609-0226

Craiglist
Clark County
portland.craigslist.org/search/clk/gms

Estate Sales Net Vancouver
estatesales.net

Garage Sale Finder
garagesalefinder.com

GSALR Garage Sale By Map
gsalr.com

Marketplace Garage Sale
Vancouver, Washington
facebook.com/marketplace/108565719168398/garagesale

NW Largest Garage Sale
Apr–Jul – Nov
nwgsales.com
360-907-5919

Yard/Garage Sale
Vancouver
facebook.com/profile.
php?id=100057512055404
360-260-4968

Yard Sale Search – Vancouver
yardsalesearch.com/garage-sales-
vancouver-wa.html

Gardens

A big factor in the Vancouver location being chosen to become a primary hub of the HBC was that it was determined to be an ideal area for raising crops and livestock. This proved to be true and in a few short years HBC farms were producing the largest and best crops and livestock in the Pacific Northwest.
Today gardens continue to flourish throughout the city.

Add Notes

Garden Clubs

Community Garden Club of Camas-Washougal
1718 SE 7th Ave, Camas
gardenclubofcamaswashougal.org

Washington State Federation of Garden Clubs
wagardenclubs.com

Community

Community gardens
An opportunity to have a small garden plot to grow whatever you want for a season usually starting in April and ending in November. There are a limited number of 10x10 and 20x20 garden plots for a small seasonal fee ranging between $20 to $50 depending upon age and other eligibility factors.
cityofvancouver.us/parksrecculture/
page/community-gardens
360-487-7100

Campus Garden
Campus Dr and 65th Ave

Ellsworth Road Garden
10916 SE 10th St

Fruit Valley Park Garden
31st St and Fruit Valley Rd

LeRoy Haagen Community Park Garden
NE 9th St, west of NE 136th Ave

Marshall Community Park Garden
1009 E. McLoughlin Blvd

Heritage Farm Community Gardens
88 plots, each 20 x 20 feet, are available on a yearly basis for $75. A limited number of disabled-accessible plots are available. Each plot includes water and use of some tools.
1919 NE 78th St
extension.wsu.edu/clark/community-gardens
Email: Jodee Nickel @ WSU Clark County Extension
564-397-5713

Natural Gardens at Pacific Community Park
NE 18th St and NE 172nd Ave
Email: Jodee Nickel @ WSU Clark County Extension
564-397-5713

Clark County Community Gardens
Clark County manages community gardens at Pacific Park in east Vancouver. There are 19 plots, each 4 x 16 feet, that are rented out annually. Gardeners are required to use natural gardening practices (e.g., no herbicides, pesticides, etc.). In February, we begin the process of renewing and assigning garden plots for the growing season. If you would like to placed on the waiting list, please email us at communitygarden@clark.wa.gov.

NE 18th St and NE 172nd Ave
clarkgreenneighbors.org/en/community-gardens

Events

Home & Garden Idea Fair
clarkpublicutilities.com/event/home-garden-idea-fair

Master Gardener Foundation of Clark County
mgfcc.com/events.html

Natural Garden Tour
clarkgreenneighbors.org/en/natural-garden-tour

Historical Gardens

The first large garden in the Northwest was planted at Fort Vancouver in 1828, under the direction of Dr. John McLoughlin.
The Hudson's Bay Company was the first to introduce non-native species of agricultural crops from Europe and "stowaway" seeds that were brought in with the ships' cargo. Apples, grape vines, vegetables, and a variety of flowers were neatly planted between walking paths for the officers and guests;

they also enjoyed the yield of the garden during elaborate British- and French-Canadian-prepared meals at the Factor house.

Grain crops were planted in larger fields for livestock feeding, ground into flour for baking, and with a small portion of the crops designated for beer and even some whiskey production.

Fort Vancouver Garden

Garden volunteers spend endless hours re-creating the heritage garden using only vintage seeds and plantings that were in use at the time.

Fort Vancouver National Historic Site
612 E Reserve St
https://www.nps.gov/places/fova-garden.htm
360-816-6230
See also:
nps.gov/fova/learn/historyculture/thegarden.htm

At the end of each season, the seeds are carefully harvested for replanting and available in the Fort Vancouver Bookstore.
1501 E Evergreen Blvd
friendsfortvancouver.org
360-816-6216
Add Notes

Hulda Klager Lilac Gardens

A National Historic site that honors the work of famed lilac developer Hulda Klager with the restored 1880s Victorian farmhouse and country garden. The home and gift shop is open only during lilac days in May.
115 S Pekin Rd, Woodland
lilacgardens.com

Resources - Garden

Gardening in Washington State–WSU

An extensive statewide resource maintained by the College of Agriculture, Human, and Natural Resources at WSU.
gardening.wsu.edu

Heritage Trees

Designated trees over 36 inches in diameter in Clark County represent a species or relate to a historical event or time. Currently, 8 such trees are listed by the WSU Extension Clark County Master Gardener program. Visit the website to view a video and connect to pictures and location of these majestic trees.
extension.wsu.edu/clark/heritage-tree
564-397-5738

Home Vegetable Gardening in Washington State

A free 28-page manual for home vegetable gardening by the WSU Extension Home Garden Series. It covers everything from site-specific growing conditions such as temperature maps, types of gardening, as well as harvesting and storage of crop produce. t.ly/8M84 (pdf)

Master Gardener Foundation of Clark County

The Master Gardener Program offers a variety of ways to get your questions answered about residential gardening, landscaping, soil testing, and species identification.
Answer Clinic: email: mganswerclinic@clark.wa.gov. or mgfcc.com/index.html
564-397-5711

See also: extension.wsu.edu/clark/master-gardeners

National Gardening Association

If you are new to gardening or just need more information, this resource is helpful for beginner and expert gardeners alike. A database of 700,000 plants and nearly half a million photos comprise contributions from over a million members.
garden.org

Native Plant Life

Love this! A two-page pictorial of Vancouver native plants that shows bloom time and the wildlife attraction for each plant. Produced by the City of Vancouver Water Resource Center. pdf-t.ly/k0Vj

Natural Gardens Pacific Community Park

A demonstration garden for natural plants that will grow in the Vancouver area.
NE 18th St and NE 172nd Ave
360-397-6060, ext 5738

Nature Scaping of SW Washington

This is a year-round garden and education center for learning garden concepts that attract birds, butterflies, and wildlife to residential gardens with ten themed gardens. (Entrance, Collector's, Cottage, Flying Flowers, Homestead, Hummingbird Place, Manor, NW Birdhaven, Natives, and Water Wise) are planted with almost 200 different species and varieties of perennials, representing 30 or more plant families.

The gardens are free and open daily from dawn to dusk.
11000 NE 149th St, Brush Prairie
naturescaping.org
360-737-1160

WSU Garden Publications
More information than you'll ever need, but make yourself an expert by reading just a few of these free resources, such as "A Home Gardener's Guide to Soils and Fertilizers" or "Backyard Composting," as well as manuals on agriculture, general gardening, plants, pests and diseases, and more.
pubs.extension.wsu.edu/gardening

Shops & Greenhouses

Aitken's Salmon Creek Garden
Family-owned iris and orchid nursery in business since 1978. Terry Aitken has received top awards for his work in iris hybridizing with currently over 200 iris varieties for sale and over 5,000 orchids in his greenhouse. Display garden is open from late April till first week of July.
608 NW 119th St
flowerfantasy.net
360-573-4472

All Season Plants
Plants, garden decor, and seasonal gifts.
7920 NE 6th Ave
allseasonplants.com
360-567-4000

Cascade Greenhouse
A local, family-owned greenhouse (35 years and counting). Their specialty is hanging baskets, but they have a variety of annuals, perennials, veggie starts, herbs,

sedums, succulents, house plants, and nursery stock.
6005 NE 139th St
cascadegreenhouse.net
360-892-9494

Chapman's Greenhouse and Nursery
Established in 1982, they are now a multigenerational family business offering a variety of bedding plants, hanging baskets, perennials, and vegetables.
14002 NE 117th Ave
chapmansgreenhouseandnursery.com
360-892-1405

Dennis 7 Dees
(formerly Shorty's Garden Center)
10006 Mill Plain Blvd
dennis7dees.com/vancouver-garden-center
360-892-7880

Orchards Feed
10902 NE Rosewood Ave
orchardsfeed.com/home.html
360-892-3001

Trans Nursery and Landscaping
5105 NE St. Johns Rd
transnursery.com
360-699-0900

Yard and Garden Land
My go-to place for great plants and gift gardening ideas.
1501 NE 102nd St
yardngardenland.com
360-573-7172

Geocaching

Geocaching is a treasure hunt activity that involves finding small caches that are hidden in parks, along streets, country roads, or anywhere across the globe. There are millions of caches hidden worldwide waiting for you to find and, of course, once you are hooked, you can create your own and spread the fun.
geocaching.com

Geocaching North Vancouver
This is a basic list of favorite North Vancouver geocaches. The website says there are roughly 4,817 geocaches around Portland, OR.
geocaching.com/bookmarks/view.aspx?guid=38673c97-0739-485d-add9-6c508cacf3dc

Trail Link
Geocaching Trails & Maps Washington
Top-rated geocaching trails with descriptions, maps, photos, and reviews.
traillink.com/stateactivity/wa-geocaching-trails
Add Notes

Golf

In 1903, a Portland golf professional laid out a nine-hole course on the Barracks grounds and gave lessons, it's said, to General Funston among others developing their expert swings.

In 1925, a nine-hole course was created along the banks of Salmon Creek that lasted only about ten years because of the Great Depression. The Reflector in 2017 shared in article from the Clark County History – 2011 – Volume XLVII that offers a fun read about these early golf days in Vancouver.
thereflector.com/stories/a-hole-in-one-or-a-triple-bogey,41935

Courses & Clubs

Camas Meadows Golf Course
4105 NW Camas Meadows Dr, Camas
camasmeadows.com
360-833-2000

Club Green Meadows
7703 NE 72nd Ave
clubgreenmeadows.com
360-256-1510

Fairway Village Golf Course
15509 SE Fernwood Dr
fairwayvillagegolf.com
360-254-9325

Orchard Hills Golf Club
605 39th St, Washougal
ohgcc.com
360-835-5444

Pinecrest Golf Course Par 3
2415 NW 143rd St
pinecrestgc.net
360-573-2051

Royal Oaks Country Club
(members only)
8917 NE Fourth Plain Blvd
royaloaks.net
360-256-1250

Disc Golf

Not to be confused with those little white balls one hits with a club, disc golf is basically throwing frisbees at a target with rules "similar to golf," in that there is a number of targets and one moves from one target to the next. For competitions, players may use as many as 20 different discs for different types of play. It's a great sport for exercise, with the typical course requiring a mile or more of walking.

Disc Golf Course 1st Tee
14900 NE Salmon Creek Ave

Glenwood Disc Golf Course
12201 NE 72nd Ave
glenwoodcc.org/mission/local/disc-golf
360-571-3300

Leverich Park Disc Golf Course
4209 NE Leverich Park Way
pdga.com/course-directory/course/leverich-park-disc-golf-course
360-487-8311

Mini Golf

Bazooka Battle Putt Putt
7120 NE Hwy 99
360-694-4719

Cosmic Miniature Golf
5101 NE 112th Ave
360-885-2368

Safari Mini Golf
8700 NE Vancouver Mall Dr, #191
laserblasters.com
360-326-2343

Ranges - Golf

Camas Meadows Driving Range
4105 NW Camas Meadows Dr, Camas
camasmeadows.com
360-833-2000

Salmon Creek Golf Range
14205 NE 3rd Ct
westsidegolfacademy.com
360-573-2565

Vanco Golf Range
703 N Devine Rd
facebook.com/vancogolfrange
360-693-8811

Westside Golf Range
14205 NE 3rd Ct
facebook.com/WestsideGolfRange
360-573-2565

Gymnastics

Gymnastics is mostly an indoor sport that includes physical exercises requiring balance, strength, flexibility, agility, coordination, dedication, and endurance. Different types of gymnastics include artistic, rhythmic, trampoline, power, and acrobatic.

Kids Club Fun & Fitness
13914 NW 3rd Ct
kidsclub4fun.com
360-546-5437

Naydenov Gymnastics & Fun
5313 NE 94th Ave
6315 NE 63rd St (Open 2023)
ngymnastics.com
360-944-4444

Northpointe Gymnastics
6707 NE 117th Ave, Ste D100
northpointe-gym.com
360-254-7958

SWAG – Gymnastics
3000 Columbia House Blvd, Unit 120
swag-gymnastics.com
360-326-4724

The Little Gym
3000 SE 164th Avenue Unit 111
thelittlegym.com/vancouverwa
360-828-8492

Vancouver Elite
240 NE 3rd Ave, Camas
vegagym.com
360-834-7424

Horseback Riding

Vancouver

Renaissance Farms
24920 NE 14th St
facebook.com/RenaissanceFarmsEquestrian
360-852-3250

Son Rise Ranch
24003 NE 44th St
sonriseranchwa.com
360-834-9103

Clark County

Bar UK River Ranch
30906 NE 26th Ave, La Center
barukriverranch.com
360-513-4457

Brindle Ridge Farm
3000 NW 299th St, Ridgefield
brindleridgefarms.com
360-521-0679

Clark County Saddle Club
11407 NE 174th St, Battle Ground
clarkcountysaddleclub.com

Cantera Equestrian
1613 NE 259th St Ridgefield
canteraequestrian.com
360-607-0493

Quarry Ridge Farm
25604 NE Manley Rd, Battle Ground
quarryridgefarm.com/index.html
360-909-8605

Ice Skating

Mountain View Ice Arena
14313 SE Mill Plain Blvd
mtviewice.com
360-896-8700

Karaoke/Open Mic

Karaoke is a Japanese name for singing to music. Lots of folks do this in the car, shower or while working but it's fun to take it up a notch and do it with a listening audience. Some of us may need a drink or two and some good "go for it" push from friends before tackling the mic . . .

Back Alley Bar & Grill
Karaoke Fri-Sat
6503 E Mill Plain Blvd, Ste E
thebackalleyonline.com
360-694-6873

Cedar Room
6300 NE Hwy 99
360-694-8872

Donnell's Bar
813 Main St
facebook.com/DonnellsBar
360-984-6720

Husted's Hazel Dell Lanes
Karaoke Wed-Sat
6300 NE Hwy 99
hazeldelllanes.com
360-694-8364

Latte Da Coffee House & Wine Bar
Special events.
205 E 39th St
lattedacoffeehouse.com
360-448-7651

Orchards Tap
Karaoke 7 nights a week.
10514 NE Fourth Plain Blvd
orchardstap.net
360-891-5917

Silver Star Saloon
6718 NE Fourth Plain Blvd
silver-star-saloon.business.site
360-694-5742

Spot Bar & Grill
Karaoke Sun-Thu 7pm-9pm
7225 NE Fourth Plain Blvd
facebook.com/thespotvancouver
360-256-1110

TJ's Cascade Bar & Grill
15000 SE Mill Plain Blvd
tjscascadebarandgrill.com

Kayaking

Peach Beach Rentals
4503 SE 164th Ave
peach-beach-rentals.business.site
360-356-8629

Ridgefield Kayak Rentals
5 Mill St, Ridgefield
ridgefieldkayak.com
360-727-4520

Sweetwater SUP Rentals
341 NW Lake Rd, Camas
sweetwatersuprentals.com
360-609-1212

WaSupNW
wasupnw.com
360-787-8483

Laser Tag

Crossfire Lasertag
Mobile laser tag – comes to your party, church event, etc.
crossfirelasertag.com

Laser Blasters
8700 NE Vancouver Mall Dr, Ste 191
laserblasters.com

Libraries

"The very first library in the Pacific Northwest was established by the Hudson's Bay Company in 1833 at Fort Vancouver."
History of Fort Vancouver Libraries
fvrl.org/history

Vancouver

Fort Vancouver Regional Library (FVRL)
Besides books, the library also offers many other programs for free or with a free library card.
Online learning resources from more than 1,000 programming partners. Learning and exam preparation resources; e-books, e-audio, magazines, videos. Library events both virtual and in person.

Cascade Park
600 NE 136th Ave
fvrl.org/loc/cp
360-906-5000 (all FBRL Libraries)

Three Creeks
800-C Tenney Rd
fvrl.org/loc/tc
360-906-4790

Vancouver Community Library
901 C St
fvrl.org/loc/vancouver
360-906-5000

Vancouver Mall
8700 NE Vancouver Mall Dr, Ste 285
fvrl.org/loc/tm
360-906-5000

Clark County

Battle Ground
1207 SE 8th Way, Battle Ground
fvrl.org/loc/bg
360-906-5000

Goldendale
131 West Burgen St, Goldendale
fvrl.org/loc/gd
888-546-2707

La Center
1411 NE Lockwood Creek Rd, La Center
fvrl.org/loc/lc
360-906-4760

North Bonneville
214 CBD Mall N (inside City Hall), North Bonneville
fvrl.org/loc/nb
888-546-2707

North Bonneville

214 CBD Mall N (inside City Hall),
North Bonneville
fvrl.org/loc/nb
888-546-2707

Ridgefield

210 N Main Ave, Ridgefield
fvrl.org/loc/ri
360-906-4770

Stevenson

120 NW Vancouver Ave, Stevenson
fvrl.org/loc/st
509-427-5471

Washougal

1661 C St, Washougal
fvrl.org/loc/wa
360-906-4860

White Salmon Valley

77 NE Wauna Ave, White Salmon
fvrl.org/loc/ws
509-493-1132

Woodland

770 Park St, Woodland
fvrl.org/loc/wd
360-906-4830

Yacolt Express

105 E Yacolt Rd, Yacolt
fvrl.org/loc/yt
360-906-5000

Yale Express

11700 Lewis River Rd, Ariel
fvrl.org/loc/ye
800-921-6211

Little Free Library

Free libraries can be found throughout Vancouver. You will find them on the streets, in small shops, laundromats, and even in restaurants, donut shops, coffee shops, and other businesses. Some of them are registered with Little Free Libraries (see below) or simply as an act of kindness and sharing as a part of being neighborly.

Little Free Libraries

littlefreelibrary.org/ourmap

Libraries–Other

Clark College Library

Lewis D. Cannell Library
1933 Fort Vancouver Way
library.clark.edu
360-992-2151

Clark County Law Library

Clark County Courthouse, 1200 Franklin St, first floor
clark.wa.gov/law-library

Clark County Museum

Three collections of unpublished manuscripts and literary artifacts: original, digital, and special.
Brautigan Library
1511 Main St
thebrautiganlibrary.org/index.html
360-993-5679

Military Groups & Associations

American Legion

The American Legion Smith-Reynolds, Post 14
americanlegion14.com
360-696-2579

Salmon Creek American Legion Post 176
post176.com
360-573-2331

General

Buffalo Soldiers of Portland, OR
facebook.com/Buffalo-Soldiers-Pacific-NW-Chapter-143006529714199

Clark County Veterans Assistance Center
1305 Columbia St
360-693-7030

Clark County Veterans Monument
Located in a corner of the Fort Vancouver Park near the Barracks.

Vancouver Barracks Military Association
Formed by a group of veterans in 2011 to interpret the history of the Vancouver Barracks. Membership open to all.
vbma.us

Vancouver Barracks National Cemetery
"Vancouver Barracks was established in 1849 as the first U.S. Army post in the Pacific Northwest. It closed as an active post in 2011. The cemetery contains more than 1,500 occupied grave sites, including U.S. military personnel, civilians, foreign personnel, German and Italian POWs, Native Americans, and Unknowns." Press Release
cem.va.gov/pressreleases/Vancouver_Barracks_Post_Cemetery_transferred_to_VA.asp

VFW

VFW Post 400
400 N Andresen Rd
vfw7824.org
360-254-0155

Model Trains

Columbia Gorge Model Railroad
2505 N Vancouver Ave, Portland, Or
facebook.com/cgmrc

National Model Railroad Association
nmra.org

Southwest Washington Model Railroaders Club
2700 E 28th St
facebook.com/Southwest-Washington-Model-Railroaders-147237705342435
360-737-6780

Museums

Clark County Historical Museum

Tue-Sat 11am-4pm **and** 1st Fri 5pm-8pm

Adults $5, youth (ages 5-18) $4, students (18+) Active military, first responders, essential health care workers free; free parking and meter parking. FVRL offers free pass per library card once a month.
1511 Main St
cchmuseum.org
360-993-5679

North Clark Historical Museum

2nd & 4th Saturday
Free
21416 399th St Amboy
northclarkhistoricalmuseum.org
360-247-5800

Pearson Air Museum

Tue-Sat 9am-4pm
Free
1115 E 5th St
nps.gov/fova/planyourvisit/pearsonairmuseum.htm
360-816-6232

Veterans Museum

Vancouver VA Medical Center, 14 Plain Blvd

Wendel Museum of Animal Conservation

A collection of animals displayed from around the world for people to learn about the important role hunters play in conserving wildlife and their habitats. Tours by appt
8303 SE Evergreen Hwy
wendelmuseum.com
360-241-9646

Padel Ball

Firstenburg Community Center

700 NE 136th Ave
cityofvancouver.us/firstenburg
360-487-7001

Padelhorn

See Pickelball entry below
9210 NE 62nd Ave Bld A Ste 110
padelhorn.com

Pickelball

Firstenburg Community Center

700 NE 136th Ave
cityofvancouver.us/firstenburg
360-487-7001

Padelhorn

With 4 pickleball courts they are the first dedicated indoor pickleball courts in the Vancouver/Portland area. All bookings done through Playtomic - app recommended.
playtomic.io
9210 NE 62nd Ave Bld A Ste 110
padelhorn.com

Rock Climbing

Jim Parsley Community Center
2901 Falk Rd (entrance off Plomondon Road)
jpcc.vansd.org
360-313-1060

Source Climbing
1118 Main St
sourceclimbing.com
360-694-9096

Scavenger Hunts

City of Vancouver
Parks Scavenger Hunt
Free
cityofvancouver.us/parksrecculture/page/parks-scavenger-hunt

Visit Vancouver WA Scavenger Hunt
Free
visitvancouverwa.com/passes

Crazy Dash–Vancouver
$20 starting ticket
crazydash.com/Locations/Vancouver-WA

Event Brite–Vancouver
$19.99-$34.99 (per team or group, any size)
eventbrite.com/e/one-team-scavenger-hunt-vancouver-tickets-111103222730?aff=ebdssbdestsearch

Operation City Quest
$20 starting ticket
operationcityquest.com/Locations/Vancouver-WA

Puzzling Adventures Vancouver
$49 per team
t.ly/CGT4

Stray Boots Vancouver
Team Building
$30 starting
strayboots.com/usa/vancouver-wa-hunts

Wacky Walks Vancouver
$20 starting ticket
wackywalks.com/Locations/Vancouver-WA

Zombies Scavengers Vancouver
$42 starting ticket
zombiescavengers.com/Locations/Vancouver-WA

Shooting Sports

Archery

Archery World
6300 NE St. James Rd Ste 102
archeryworld.net
360-693-7510

Clubs

Clark Country Gun Club
820 NE 192 Ave
clarkcountygunclub.com
360-326-8341

Clark Rifles
Not accepting new members
25115 Northeast Rawson Road
Brush Prairie
clarkrifles.org
360-944-1118

Vancouver Rifle and Pistol Club
12211 NE 76th St
vancouverrifle.com
360-253-9651 (message only)

Vancouver Trap and Gun Club
11100 NE 76th St
vancouvertrapandgunclub.com
360-892-5005

Ranges

English Pit Shooting Range
820 NE 192 Ave
englishpit.com
360-326-8341

Safe Fire
4857 NW Lake Rd, Suite 210 Camas
shootatsafefire.com
360-834-7233

Skateboarding

Endeavor Park
NE Angelo Dr. and Four Seasons Ln
cityofvancouver.us/parksrecculture/
page/endeavour-park

Gretchen Fraser Neighborhood Park
Mill Plain Blvd. at 155th Ave
cityofvancouver.us/parksrecculture/
page/gretchen-fraser-neighborhood-
park

Northwest Skater–Vancouver
2401 E Fourth Plain Blvd
northwestskater.com/vancouverdt.
html

Pacific Community Park
1515 NE 164th Ave
cityofvancouver.us/parksrecculture/
page/gretchen-fraser-neighborhood-
park

Water Works Park
Fourth Plain and Ft. Vancouver Way
cityofvancouver.us/parksrecculture/
page/water-works-park

Soccer

Christensen Soccer Field
Home of the Clark College Penguins men's and women's soccer teams.
clarkpenguins.com/facilities/kim-
christensen-field/28

Luke Jensen Sports Park
Baseball and soccer, primarily used by Vancouver West Soccer Club.
clark.wa.gov/public-works/luke-
jensen-sports-park

Vancouver West Soccer Club

Soccer Fields for Vancouver West Soccer Club *
vancouverwestsc.org

Columbia River High School
800 NW 99th St
river.vansd.org
360-313-3900

Eisenhower Elementary School
9201 NW 9th Ave
eisenhower.vansd.org
360-313-1700

Jason Lee Middle School
8500 NW 9th Ave
jlee.vansd.org
360-313-3500

Lake Shore Elementary School
9300 NW 21st Ave
lakeshore.vansd.org
360-313-2250

Lincoln Elementary School
4200 NW Daniels St
lincoln.vansd.org
360-313-2300

Luke Jensen Sports Complex
4000 NE 78th St
clark.wa.gov/public-works/luke-jensen-sports-park
360-397-2285

Memory Field Soccer Field
1007 E Mill Plain Blvd

Vancouver School of Arts and Academics
3101 Main St
arts.vansd.org
360-313-4600

Washington Timbers
Portland Timbers FC Alliance soccer club for kids playing at all levels aged 5-18.
washingtontimbers.com

Swimming
Clubs
Cascade Athletic Club
Swimming and lessons.
16096 SE 15th St
cascadeac.com/vancouver
360-597-1100

Columbia River Swim Team
teamunify.com/team/oscrst/page/home

Touchmark Health Club
2911 SE Village Loop
britishswimschool.com/locations/us/wa/vancouver/touchmark-health-club
360-210-1111

Clark County Parks
Daybreak Regional Park
26401 NE Daybreak Rd, Battle Ground
clark.wa.gov/public-works/day-break-regional-park-and-boat-launch
360-397-2285

Frenchman's Bar Regional Park
9612 NW Lower River Rd
clark.wa.gov/public-works/french-mans-bar-regional-park
360-397-2285

Haapa Boat Launch
43511 NE Haapa Rd, Woodland
clark.wa.gov/public-works/haapa-boat-launch

Lewisville Regional Park
26411 NE Lewisville Hwy, Battle Ground
clark.wa.gov/publicworks/parks/lewisville.html
360-397-2285

Moulton Falls Regional Park
27781 NE Lucia Falls Road, Yacolt
clark.wa.gov/public-works/moulton-falls-regional-park

Salmon Creek Regional Park-Klineline Pond
Lifeguards (usually) Jul–Memorial Day, life jacket loaner station.
1112 NE 117th St
clark.wa.gov/public-works/salmon-creek-regional-park/klineline-pond

Vancouver Lake Regional Park
6801 NW Lower River Rd
clark.wa.gov/public-works/vancou-ver-lake-regional-park
360-397-2285

Clark State Park

Battle Ground Lake State Park
   Shallow swim area for children.
18002 NE 249th St, Battle Ground
parks.state.wa.us/472/Battle-Ground-Lake
360-687-4621

Community Centers

Firstenburg Community Center
One adult must be in the water for every three children under age seven.
700 NE 136th Ave
cityofvancouver.us/fcc
360-487-7001

Jim Parsley Community Center
Public swimming, lessons, and lifeguard training.
Boys & Girls Club,
4100 Plomondon St
jpcc.vansd.org
360-313-1060

Marshall/Luepke Community Center
Children 15 years and under must be accompanied in the pool by someone age 16+
Public swimming, lessons.
1009 E. McLoughlin Blvd
cityofvancouver.us/parksrecculture/page/marshall-center-aquatics
360-487-7100

Propstra Aquatic Center
605 N Devine Rd
vansd.org/propstra-aquatic-center
360-313-3625

Lessons

Cascade Athletic Club
(see Swimming - clubs)

Harmony Swim School
facebook.com/harmonyswimschool

Kids Club Fun & Fitness
13914 NW 3rd Ct
kidsclub4fun.com
360-546-5437

Clark County Family YMCA
11324 NE 51st Circle
ymcacw.org/locations/clark-county-family-ymca
360-885-9622

Tennis

Clark College Tennis Courts
Four courts.
Portland Tennis League,
1850 Fort Vancouver Way
tennisportland.com/court_detail/
vancouver-clark-college

PNW Tennis Center
5300 E 18th St
pnwtenniscenters.com/vancouver
360-773-5038

Clark County, Washington, Parks
clark.wa.gov/public-works/clark-county-parks

Columbia Tech Center Park
8am-5pm
1498 SE Tech Center Place, Ste 150
columbiatechcenter.com/nature-play

Theaters

Take a break from the day to day and step into another world through live theater performance or big screen movies. Vancouver has a blend of old and new venues for you to check out.

AMC CLASSIC Mill Plain 8
11700 SE 7th St
amctheatres.com/movie-theatres/seattle-tacoma/amc-classic-mill-plain-8
360-839-2981

AMC Vancouver Mall 23
8700 NE Vancouver Mall Drive
amctheatres.com/movie-theatres/seattle-tacoma/amc-vancouver-mall-23
360-839-2980

Kiggins Theatre
Historical theater with 136 seats, from 1937. A unique and fun experience.
1011 Main St
kigginstheatre.com
360-816-0352

Magenta Theater
Live performances.
1108 Main St
magentatheater.com
360-949-3098

Regal Cascade
1101 SE 160th Ave
regmovies.com/theatres/regal-cascade-imax-rpx
844-462-7342

Regal Cinema 99
9010 NE Hwy 99
regmovies.com/theatres/regal-cinema-99
844-462-7342

Regal City Center
801 C St
regmovies.com/theatres/regal-city-center
360-949-3098

Regal Vancouver Plaza
7800 NE Fourth Plain
regmovies.com/theatres/regal-vancouver-plaza
844-462-7342

Volleyball

Clark County Indoor Sports Center
16311 NE 15th St
ccisoccer.com
360-604-4487

Frenchman's Bar Regional Park
   Has 8 sand volleyball courts with the nets typically up between May 15 and Sep 15. Courts can be reserved by the hour or by the day for a fee. When not reserved courts are open to first-come, first-serve basis.
9612 NW Lower River Road
clark.wa.gov/public-works/french-mans-bar-regional-park
564-3972285

O'Connell Sports Center
   Home to the Clark College Penguins, OSC includes a gymnasium where college basketball and volleyball games are played.
1933 Fort Vancouver Way
clarkpenguins.com/facilities/o-con-nell-sports-center/8

One Ohana Volleyball
   Volleyball training facility focusing on the mental game, speed, agility, jump and skill training.
7500 NE 16th Ave #1a
oneohanavolleyball.com
360-558-3303

Volunteering

   Sharing one's time and talent is a wonderful way to build a better community and at the same time enrich your own life with new friends, activity and meaningfulness. You can make a difference.

City of Vancouver

Volunteer Programs
   Volunteer programs including litter removal, parks & recreation, adopt a park, urban forestry, neighbors on watch, fire corps, annual trail count, water center, and neighborhoods.
cityofvancouver.us/cmo/page/volunteer-programs

Clark County Food Bank
6502 NE 47th Ave
clarkcountyfoodbank.org
360-693-0939

Fort Vancouver Regional Library
fvrl.org/volunteer
360-906-5000

Vancouver Public Schools
   Connect with a school that is close to your home or place of work or choose an age level of students you prefer to work with. *(See website for list of schools and locations).*
vansd.org/volunteer

Other

A Caring Closet
Provides gently used medical equipment at no cost. Volunteers pick up, deliver and coordinate equipment.
acaringcloset.org/volunteer
360-258-0039

American Red Cross
Find local volunteer opportunities.
redcross.org

Share Volunteer Center
Community building through relationships, advocation for equal housing, food and more.
sharevancouver.org
360-448-2121

Retirement Connection
List of volunteer organizations in the Vancouver/Clark County area.
retirementconnection.com/listings/
volunteer-opportunities-community-government-vancouver

PeaceHealth SW Medical Center
Volunteers assist in nearly every area of the medical center.
peacehealth.org/hospitals/south-west-medical-center/volunteer
360-696-5069

Volunteer Match
Find volunteer opportunities by location.
volunteermatch.org

Walking Trails

These trails are well marked, and most are hard surfaced enough for wheelchairs and baby strollers. Many allow dogs on a leash, which is a necessity for the enjoyment and safety of others and wildlife.

Most of the longer trails can easily be divided into 1 and 2 mile walks with different start and stop points.

City of Vancouver
Offers a 20 mile network of trails for walkers, runners, bikers

and others to enjoy. An extensive interactive map of the trails lists parks and trails with information on locations and amenities.

cityofvancouver.us/parksrecculture/page/parks-trails

Burnt Bridge Creek Trail

An 8 mile trail that is flat paved for biking & foot traffic. It wanders through open grasslands & wooded areas with numerous access points for smaller walks.

1617 N Devine Rd

Columbia River Renaissance Trail

A 5-mile riverfront trail.

cityofvancouver.us/parksrecculture/page/columbia-river-renaissance-trail-5-miles

Discovery Historic Loop Trail-Trail

A 2.3-mile trail through Fort Vancouver and downtown Vancouver.

E Evergreen Blvd at Officers Row
cityofvancouver.us/parksrecculture/page/discovery-historic-loop-trail-2-miles

Ellen Davis Trail

A 2-mile multipurpose trail through the neighborhoods.

2109 NE 60th St
wta.org/go-hiking/hikes/ellen-davis-trail

Evergreen Highway Trail at Columbia Springs

cityofvancouver.us/parksrecculture/page/evergreen-highway-trail-columbia-springs

Frenchman's Bar Hiking Trail

traillink.com

Trail Link

List of 39 trails in the Vancouver area.

traillink.com

Add Notes

Navigating Vancouver's Streets

Located along the Columbia River's northern banks, Vancouver measures 52.45 square miles and is longer in area than it is wide. Its shape resembles a "V" lying on its side or, for the more imaginative, a lazy rabbit lying on its side with ears extended.

The 19th-century city depended on the Columbia River for transportation, which explains why its origins are along the riverbank, before it expanded north.

The Hudson's Bay Company (HBC) established a fur-trading post in 1825, which became known as Fort Vancouver. When the U.S. Army arrived in 1849, it built Vancouver Barracks next to the trading post and, after the HBC abandoned the fort for stations in British Columbia, it took over the facility.

Most of the early street names in this section of town pay tribute to **HBC**: Mill Plain, 4th Plain, and McLoughlin Blvd, for example; or the **U.S. Army:** MacArthur Blvd, Andresen Rd, and Grand Blvd (originally Grant Blvd after Ulysses S. Grant). In the town's old section, the streets sometimes run north and south and sometimes east and west. In early days, a road was called a street no matter which direction it took.

Basically, all numbered "streets," such as 5th St, 15th St, etc., run east and west; and "named streets" and alphabet ("a, b, c …") streets run north and south.

In the town's historic section, all boulevards mostly run east and west, including Evergreen Blvd, Mill Plain Blvd, McLoughlin Blvd ,and 4th Plain Blvd. The exceptions are St. John's Blvd and Macarthur Blvd, which run north and south.

When Clark County took over the assigning of roadways, the historic streets were allowed to remain. Going forward, they followed state and federal guidelines for naming streets.

Thus if a main roadway goes east and west it is a street and if a main road goes north and south it is an avenue.

Public Transportation

To and From Portland Airport (PDX) to Vancouver

A taxi ride is basically 12.6 miles from PDX to Vancouver.

Portland Taxi
portlandtaxi.net
503-256-5400

Radio Cab
radiocab.net/#/booking
503-227-1212

Vancouver Cab
Local owned; 15 years in service
facebook.com/vancouvercab
360-737-3333

App-Based Rideshares

Lyft
Est. $30-$35
lyft.com

Uber
Est. $24-$38
uber.com/global/en/airports/pdx

General Shuttles

Portlandia Airport Shuttle LLC
Est. $50
portlandia-shuttle.com
503-984-0354

Vancouver Bus Service

C-Tran provides bus service throughout Clark County service area which includes Express commuter service to downtown Portland and Marquam Hill; connections to the nearest light rail station, and five service areas for on-demand rideshare service within the city limits of Camas, Washougal, La Center, Ridgefield and Vancouver.

Visit their website for fares, instructions on how to ride and other features available.

mail.c-tran.com

Routes: mail.c-tran.com/routes

Maps: mail.c-tran.com/system-maps/c-tran-full-system-map

Add Notes

Portland International Airport

17 airlines at **PDX** serve Portland/Vancouver Metro

The airport is open 24 hours, 7 days per week.
Airline ticket counter and checkpoint hours vary.

PDX Customer Service
Information and FAQs
Staffed daily 6am-9pm
Call or text: 503-460-4234
Text toll free: 1-877-739-4636

PDX Portland International Airport
7000 NE Airport Way Portland, OR 97218
Airportflypdx.com
503-460-4272

Air Canada
aircanada.com

flypdx.com/
NonstopDestinations?a=AC
999-689-2247

Alaska
alaskaair.com

flypdx.com/
NonstopDestinations?a=AS
800-252-7522

Allegiant
allegiantair.com

flypdx.com/
NonstopDestinations?a=G4

American Airlines
aa.com

flypdx.com/
NonstopDestinations?a=AA
800-433-7300

Boutique Air
boutiqueair.com

flypdx.com/
NonstopDestinations?a=4B

Condor
condor.com/us

flypdx.com/
NonstopDestinations?a=DE
866-960-7915

Delta
delta.com

flypdx.com/
NonstopDestinations?a=DL
866-960-7915

Frontier
flyfrontier.com

flypdx.com/
NonstopDestinations?a=F9
800-432-1359

Hawaiian
hawaiianair.com

flypdx.com/
NonstopDestinations?a=HA_
800-367-5320

149

Icelandair
icelandair.us

flypdx.com/
NonstopDestinations?a=FI
800-223-5500

jetBlue
jetblue.com

flypdx.com/
NonstopDestinations?a=B6
800-538-2583

Southwest
southwest.com

flypdx.com/
NonstopDestinations?a=WN
800-435-9792

Spirit
spirit.com

flypdx.com/
NonstopDestinations?a=NK
801-401-2200

Sun Country
suncountry.com

flypdx.com/
NonstopDestinations?a=SY
800-359-6786

United
united.com

flypdx.
comNonstopDestinations?a=UA
800-864-8331

Volaris
volaris.com

flypdx.com/
NonstopDestinations?a=Y4
855-865-2747

Westjet
westjet.com

flypdx.com/
NonstopDestinations?a=WS
888-937-8538

Add Notes

Media Connections

NEWSPAPERS
CLARK COUNTY

Camas-Washougal Post Record
425 NE 4th Avenue/P.O. Box 1013
Camas, WA 98607
camaspostrecord.com
360-834-2141

Clark Couny Live - *e-news only*
clarkcountylive.com

The Columbian
701 W 8th Street/P.O. Box 180
Vancouver, WA 98666
columbian.com
360-699-6006

The Reflector
20 NW 20th Avenue/P.O. Box 2020
Battle Ground, WA 98604
thereflector.com
360-687-5151

Vancouver Business Journal
1251 Officers Row
Vancouver, WA 98661
vbjusa.com
360-695-2442

NEWSPAPERS
PORTLAND-VANCOUVER
METRO

The Business Journal (Portland)
851 SW 6th Avenue, Ste 500
Portland, OR 97204
bizjournals.com/portland
503-219-3404

The Oregonian
1320 SW Broadway
Portland, OR 97201
oregonlive.com
360-221-8327

NEWS BUREAUS
Associated Press
121 SW Salmon Street, Ste 1450
Portland, OR 97204
ap.org
503-228-2169

MAGAZINES
CLARK COUNTY

Greet Camas Magazine
greetmag.com/locations/camas-
life-b4cf

Greet Ridgefield Magazine
greetmag.com/locations/ridgefield-
life-b345

Lacamas Magazine
405 NE 4th Ave
Camas, Washington
lacamasmagazine.com
503-308-9161

Vancouver Family Magazine
PO Box 820264
Vancouver, WA 98682
vancouverfamilymagazine.com
360-221-7762

Vancouver Visitors Travel Guide
Print or digital
visitvancouverwa.com/trip-plan-
ning/request-travel-magazine

**RADIO STATIONS
CLARK COUNTY**

Independent. Radio. Vancouver.
KXRW-FM 99.9
2906 E. Evergreen Blvd Suite #C
Vancouver, WA 98661
kxrw.fm

**Outlaw Country Radio
KIEV-LP CAMAS 102.7 FM**
Camas, WA 98607
outlaw.fm
360-216-4260

**RADIO STATIONS
PORTLAND-VANCOUVER
METRO**

OPB Channel 10
7140 SW Macadam Avenue
Portland, OR 97219
opb.org
503-293-1982

**TV STATIONS
PORTLAND-VANCOUVER
METRO**

KATU Channel 2
P.O. Box 2
Portland, OR 97207
katu.com
503-231-4222

KGW Channel 8
1501 SW Jefferson
Portland, OR 97232
kgw.com
503-226-5111

KOIN Channel 6
222 SW Columbia Street
Portland, OR 97201
koin.com
503-464-0600

KPTV FOX 12 (and KPDX 49)
14975 NW Greenbrier Parkway
Beaverton, OR 97006
kptv.com
503-548-6920

OPB Channel 10
7140 SW Macadam Avenue
Portland, OR 97219
opb.org
503-293-1982

Social Media

Connect with some favorite Vancouver & Clark County media accounts that have an active presence.

INSTAGRAM

@cchmuseum
@ConnectClarkCounty
@explorevancouverwa
@fortvancouvernps
@ipawditforward
@thecolumbian
@usavancouver (me)
@vancouver_wa
@vancouverfamily

@vancouverpoliceusa
@vanlibrary
@vdausa
@vintagebookshop
@walkvancouverus

FACEBOOK.COM/

ClarkCountyLive
ClarkCountyToday
ClarkCountyWA
VisitVancouverWA

GROUPS

groups/aroundthecouve
groups/freebuyselltradeforcoolpeople
Growing Up in Clark County, Washington *(private group but if you live in Clark County you can join)*

Community Associations

Chamber of Commerce

Camas-Washougal Chamber
422 NE 4th Ave
Camas, WA 98607
cwchamber.com
360-834-2472

Greater Vancouver Chamber
1111 Main St Suite 201
vancouverusa.com
360-694-2588

Hispanic Metropolitan Chamber
4400 NE 77th Ave Suite 275
hmccoregon.com
360-450-9044

North Clark County Chamber
360-263-4636

Ridgefield Chamber
510 Pioneer St Ste D
Ridgefield, WA 98642
ridgefieldchamberofcommerce.com
360-857-5137

Clark County Associations

Vancouver's Downtown
811 Main St
vdausa.org
360-258-1129

Uptown Association
uptownvillage.com

Neighborhood Associations of Clark County
clark.wa.gov/county-manager/neighborhood-association-directory

Neighborhood Associations of Vancouver
cityofvancouver.us/cmo/page/neighborhoods

Vancouver City Connections

Emergency Services	**9-1-1**
Police Non-Emergency Services	**3-1-1**
Community Resources	**2-1-1**
Call Before You Dig	**8-1-1**
Electricity Outage	**992-8000**

Emergency Service Requests:
Sewer Backup, Water Main Break, Traffic Signals 487-8177
(follow prompts after hours/holidays)

cityofvancouver.us/cmo/page/good-neighbor-handbook-important-contact-information

Abandoned Vehicles on Street	487-8653
Animal Control	564-397-2488
Block Party Use Permits	487-7729
Building Permits/Permit Center	487-7800
Business Licenses	487-8410 *opt. 3*
C-Tran	**695-0123**
Cable TV Complaints	487-8702
Call Before You Dig	800-795-2673
Citizen Liaison	487-8604
City General Information	487-8000
City Manager's Office	487-8600
Clark County Health Department	397-8428
Clark Public Utilities	992-3000
Clark Public Utilities Energy Assistance	992-3000
Code Compliance Hotline	487-7810
Community Mediation Service	334-5862
Department of Social and Health Services	397-0002
Fire Information	**487-7212**
Firstenburg Community Center	487-7001
Fort Vancouver Regional Library	906-5000
Graffiti (city property, right of way/parks)	487-8177
Graffiti on State of Washington Property	564-397-6118
Graffiti on Private Property	
report East Precinct	487-7500
report West Precinct	487-7355
Highway Maintenance (WSDOT)	905-2000
Housing, Emergency Shelter	
Clearing House	695-9677
Luepke Senior Center	487-7050
Marshall Community Center	487-7100
Mayor / City Council	487-8629
Northwest Natural Gas	571-5465
Office of Neighborhoods	487-8608
Operations Center Dispatch	487-8177
Parking Questions	487-8650
Parking Complaints	3-1-1
Downtown	487-8650
Parks/Right of Way Maintenance	487-8177
Portland Airport Nois	1-800-938-6647
Potholes	487-8177

Street Lights Out	487-8177
Traffic Complaint Hotline	487-7402
Urban Forestry	487-8332
Utilities (water and sewer account billing)	487-7999
Voter Registration	564-397-2345
VPD East Precinct (Dist. 3 & Dist. 4)	487-7500
VPD West Precinct (Dist. 1 & Dist. 2)	487-7355
Waste Connections	892-5370

Clark County Connections

clark.wa.gov

Assesor

clark.wa.gov/assessor

  Forms & Documents

clark.wa.gov/assessor/forms-and-documents

  Land Records

clark.wa.gov/assessor/land-records-overview

  Tax Relief Programs

clark.wa.gov/assessor/levy-overview

Animals & Pet

clark.wa.gov/community-development/animals-and-pets

Auto License

clark.wa.gov/auditor/auto-license-overview

Birth/Death Records

clark.wa.gov/public-health/birth-and-death-certificates

Business
clark.wa.gov/county-manager/starting-business

Codes & Laws
codepublishing.com/WA/ClarkCounty

Courts
clark.wa.gov/courts

Elections & Voting
clark.wa.gov/elections

Emergencies
clark.wa.gov/county/emergencies

Environment
clark.wa.gov/environment

Health
clark.wa.gov/public-health

Home & Property
clark.wa.gov/home-and-property

Jails
clark.wa.gov/sheriff/corrections-branch

Jobs & Training
clark.wa.gov/human-resources/explore-careers-clark-county

Law Library
clark.wa.gov/law-library

Licenses, Permits & Records
clark.wa.gov/county/permits-and-licenses

Marriage License
clark.wa.gov/auditor/marriage-license

Neighborhood Association
clark.wa.gov/county-manager/neighborhood-association-directory

Parks & Trails
clark.wa.gov/public-works/clark-county-parks

Police & Safety
clark.wa.gov/sheriff

Recording
clark.wa.gov/auditor/recording-guide

Recycling & Garbage
clark.wa.gov/public-health/recycling-garbage-yard-debris-collection

Social Services
clark.wa.gov/community-services

Volunteers
clark.wa.gov/volunteers

Discover More

Once you have lived here for a bit you will soon discover how much early Pacific Northwest History can be found in this area. The Fort Vancouver Website is a great place to start a deep dive into Clark County history.

nps.gov/fova/index.htm

The park service provides over a thousand pages of research and documentation providing interpretative, archeological and historical information available in pdf to read online or download. Visit my website usavancouver. com/resources for a partial listing of sources I have discovered in putting together this book. This is an ongoing project as I keep finding more!

The Columbian
Offers free or paid exclusive updates of current happenings in Vancouver. This is the primary news source for Vancouver so definitely worth consideration.

columbian.com/newsletters

Visit Vancouver WA
Anything worth checking out and seeing in the area will be covered here. Bookmark this one.

visitvancouverwa.com/blog

Friends Fort Vancouver Blog
Provides weekly updates to events, demonstrations and happenings taking place at the Fort Vancouver Bookstore and site. This is where I work three days a week and Mary Rose (military historian and Excutive Director) provides simple and engaging updates. friendsfortvancouver. org/news/news-blog

Couv Life
Rod Sager has been blogging about life in Vancouver since 2013. His writing is personal and insightful with his take on what is happening in Vancouver today.

couvlife.wordpress.com

Vancouver Washington
This is a real estate blog but if you are new to the area or thinking about moving here it has some great fact posts about life in Clark County.

living-inportlandoregon.com/blog-vancouver-washington

Clark County Conservative
This is a political blog geared to a Republican audience.

clark-county-conservative.com

USA Vancouver Blog
This is my blog offering personal insights and reflections as well as historical and area resources.

usavancouver.com/blog

Patty Grasher
Author, basic photography, book design & layout.

Dear Reader,

Did this book help you in some way? Do you have any suggestions for improvements for the next update? This is a work in progress and I would greatly appreciate to hear how I can make it better. Please leave a review. :-)

instagram.com/usavancouver/
or facebook.com/pattygrasher/

usavancouver.com

Jonathon E Kraft - Landscape photographer in Vancouver, WA. View more of his photography at Facebook page, 'Growing Up In Vancouver' or on Instagram at @johnathankraft_photography.

Contributors:
Barbara Noe Kennedy - barbaranoekennedy.com former senior editor at National Geographic Travel Publishing for outstanding editing of book.
Sasha Fedorova - @marsasha_art Ukrainian artist and map creator - continued to work even after the invasion from Russia and her migration to Poland.
Bernard McKenna - cartoonsbybernard.com providing light hearted cartoon figures Portland,OR

Warmest appreciation to **Mary Rose** at **Friends of Fort Vancouver** for continued help and guidance to historical research, general advice and continued support. Support and encouragement: Jennifer Johnson, Euli Rath, Barbara George, Barb Ries and others.

NPS Fort Vancouver Rangers: Aaron, Paula, Sarah, Ryan, Reenactors and volunteers at Fort Vancouver

The City of Vancouver for permissions and steering forward in positive direction. cityofvancouver.us

A huge thanks to **Erica Lindeman** and the marketing team at Visit Vancouver Washington for page by page reviews with corrections and suggestions for improvements which added greatly to book.

Your Vancouver Bucket List

Create your bucket list of places to explore, things to try and events to attend.

PLACES TO VISIT

THINGS I WANT TO DO

FOODS TO TASTE

EVENTS TO ATTEND

Visit Vancouver WA is the official destination marketing organization of Vancouver and the surrounding Clark County area. Visit their website for trip inspiration, maps and photos, restaurant listings, blog posts, and order your free Travel Magazine at VisitVancouverWA.com. visitvancouverwa.com.
(P.S. not endorsed by them just appreciative!)

www.ingramcontent.com/pod-product-compliance
Lightning Source LLC
Chambersburg PA
CBHW060529130626
46553CB00002B/689